protecting your teen from disturbing behavior

protecting your teen from disturbing behavior

Lee Vukich
Steve Vandegriff

Living Ink Books
An Imprint of AMG Publishers
CHATTANOOGA, TENNESSEE

Protecting Your Teen from Disturbing Behavior

Published by Living Ink Books, an imprint of AMG Publishers
6815 Shallowford Rd.
Chattanooga, Tennessee 37421

ISBN 978–089957085–3

First printing—March 2007

Cover designed by ImageWright, Chattanooga, Tennessee

Interior design and typesetting by Jennifer Ross, Chattanooga, Tennessee

Edited and Proofread by Agnes Lawless, Dan Penwell, Georgia Varozza, and Rick Steele

Printed in the United States of America
13 12 11 10 09 08 07–B–7 6 5 4 3 2 1

I dedicate this book to Pamela Jo, my wife of thirty years (as of April 9, 2007) and the mother of our three children.

—Steve Vandegriff

Contents

chapter 1

What a Teenager Looks Like

Bill Cosby, as he spoke about children in his book, *Childhood*, repeated what the French like to say, "The more things change, the more they stay the same." He continues by saying,

> These words do not, of course, refer to the birth of a butterfly, but they do refer to childhood, which has basically been the same ever since Cain decided he wanted to be an only child. The only difference between the childhood I lived and childhood today is that I didn't expect my parents to be social directors for me. I never once said I was bored, for children began to be bored only in June of 1963. I was a boy in a time when kids endlessly amused themselves, when a toddler exercise class was one toddler pounding another.
>
> Today's child tells his parents, 'You brought me here. Now entertain me.'
>
> If I ever had said these words to my father, he would have smilingly replied, 'Yes, I brought you here, and I

can take you out. I can make another one that's got to be better.'[1]

Let's take a look at what most teenagers are like. Prior to the teen years, parents will usually dote on their kids. Children do and say cute things, but before parents know it, puberty sets in. All of a sudden, those kids are changing. Sometimes the changes are for the better, but often those changes irritate parents, and even frighten them.

Physically

Physically, this *tweenager*— a child between childhood and adolescence—experiences rapid and dramatic growth. I remember a family vacation when our oldest son was sitting in the backseat of our car. When we left home, his head was below my view in the rearview mirror. Three weeks later, he was eyeball to eyeball with me in the mirror. His growth spurt was evident to relatives and friends who hadn't seen him in a while, but it was even more evident to us.

Some teenagers experience actual growing pains. The pace of their growth can be so fast that their bodies get sore. The teenagers' hands and feet first reach adult size making them clumsy. Try watching a middle-school basketball team warm up and notice that the teens lack coordination and grace. They knock over full drinking glasses, small pieces of furniture, knickknacks, and then stumble over pets and small children.

Emotionally

Emerging teenagers begin to develop a sense of personal identity and self-worth. Parents can help them find their niches, those things they do well or in which they have a strong interest. If a teenager shows interest in a team sport (basketball, volleyball, hockey) or an individual sport (snowboarding, skateboarding), the parents should allow their teenager to go as far as their interests will take them. This can be a relationship-strengthening experience between parents and teenager. Parents can make their teenager aware of good camps or conferences, help them with the costs, get them there, buy equipment, and cheer them on. Obviously, this is predicated by what is wholesome, right, and within reason.

Of course, teenagers are fickle; they change their minds and get bored easily. And parents hope that sooner than later, their teenagers will find some things that will give them their identities. As parents help to facilitate teenagers in their pursuits, this strengthens the parent/teenager relationships. This is all a part of teens striving for independence, yet still depending on their parents for the time being.

Self-conscious

While teenagers are gaining more confidence, they have one paramount concern—not global warming, not the war on terror, and not the price of gas. It's how they look! But because of their self-consciousness, they fear ridicule. Sarcastic peers target awkward teenagers for verbal abuse. Adults can act as counterbalances by offering genuine praise and encouragement. In spite of the significance of peer groups in teenagers' lives, adults are able to exert extraordinary influence with sincere compliments.

Socially

Emerging teenagers do everything enthusiastically. And the adults in their lives must be characteristically enthusiastic. Parents and adults must infuse enthusiasm in whatever they do with teenagers—and the teens will follow anywhere!

Most teens are enthusiastic but often fluctuate between being friendly and moody. So when adults think they have a solid relationship, they may turn their back on adults without warning; or when parents think they have them figured out, they go off with wild-eyed ideas. So go with the flow when maneuvering among teenagers.

Along with moodiness comes developing crushes and hero worship. As one who has raised three teenagers, I am thrilled when the youth leaders are the heroes in my teenagers' lives. I'd like to be their hero, but I know my teenagers would have a difficult time admitting that I could fulfill this role. Later on this hero role could happen, when the peer group isn't so prominent in their lives. In the meantime, I'll yield to youth ministers and youth leaders.

When dealing with the prevention of crushes, the modus operandi is to show equal attention to everyone. Be sure the good-looking and the not so attractive, the athletic and the non-physical, the popular and the not accepted, the rich and the poor get equal and undivided attention.

Mentally

Believe it or not, teenagers are beginning to think. For some, this may be a shock. At this time, teenagers move from the question of what to the *question of why*. This can be unnerving for parents and for those who work with teenagers. I'm sure my parents wondered if my brain cells as a teenager were functioning, even minimally. My sarcastic mouth with why questions, often got me in more trouble than I care to remember.

The "why" question cannot be ignored. Teenagers are learning to define their tastes, values, and preferences. So they ask why a lot. Of course, parents and adults don't always have the answers. So be honest with them and admit, "I really don't know."

This shift from non-thinking to opinions and beliefs is a great opportunity for adults to assist young people in the shaping of their tastes, values, and preferences. Some young people have moved into their adult lives with a love for alpine experiences and the great outdoors because I led them into those experiences. Other young people have pursued particular careers and ministries after I introduced them into specific professions and ministries. Still others have enrolled in Christian colleges and universities after I talked to them about those particular schools. Many young people have given their lives in the service of Christ because I introduced them to Jesus. This may sound arrogant, but it's not meant to be. I simply wanted to show that ordinary people can have a tremendous influence in helping teenagers shape their tastes, values, and preferences.

How can adults help teenagers think? One way would be to challenge them to think for themselves. Make them realize that MTV or BET doesn't think for them. Thinking requires hard work, time, and research.

The Scriptures have some things to say about thinking. They give young people an explicit grid by which to measure their thought lives.

- "For as he thinks within himself, so he is" (Prov. 23:7, NASB).
- "Therefore, prepare your minds for action" (1 Peter 1:13, NASB).
- "Finally, brothers, whatever is true, whatever is noble, whatever is right, whatever is pure, whatever is lovely, whatever is admirable—if anything is excellent or praiseworthy—think about such things" (Phil. 4:8).

We could reword the Philippians verse without losing its meaning: "Whatever is false, whatever is dishonorable, whatever is wrong, whatever is impure, whatever is ugly, whatever is of a bad reputation, don't let your minds think on such things." Without question, a believer's thought life is where the spiritual battle begins and is constantly fought.

Idealism

Teenagers' expectations of others are off the charts. For whatever reasons, they idealize the perfect parents, the perfect churches, the perfect teachers, and even the perfect world to live in. They think that the grass is greener on the other side of the fence. Unfortunately, no one or no thing can live up to their expectations. As a result, they become disappointed, even cynical of their parents, their teachers, their churches, and the world they live in.

For those living and working among teenagers, do not take their criticisms too seriously. Address them in even-tempered discussions. Teens need to know that no one is perfect—and neither are they. They need to be objective rather than subjective when people fail them. Parents and other adults will disappoint them one time or another, but that is not a justifiable reason for teens to wipe them off the radar screen.

A teen's cynicism that's brought on by idealism needs to be channeled into something productive and not just be an empty emotion. During Paul's ministry, the Berean believers "examined the Scriptures every day to see if what Paul said was true" (Acts 17:11). What a great idea for teenagers to dig into the Scriptures for themselves. First Corinthians 3:7 says, "So neither he who plants nor he who waters is anything, but only God, who makes things grow." Regardless of parents and adults' efforts, they still need the God factor. Without the Lord being involved, nothing of significance will happen.

Finally, teenagers need to be part of the solution and not just observe the problem.

- Galatians 6:10 says, "Therefore, as we have opportunity, let us do good to all people, especially to those who belong to the family of believers."

- Philippians 2:4 declares, "Each of you should look not only to your own interests, but also to the interests of others."
- Romans 16:19, states, "I want you to be wise about what is good, and innocent about what is evil."

Argumentative

Parents have told me that their teenagers argue for the sake of arguing. Exactly! Teenagers are argumentative. Remember, they're beginning to think, so arguing is their version of verbal thinking. Some adults and parents are threatened when teenagers question and argue. As unnerving as this may be, it can actually be a positive thing. Teenagers need help in distinguishing between arguing as an exercise in thinking and arguing as an exercise in trying to convince someone to their point of view. As long as it is an exercise in thinking, adults shouldn't be too concerned. But when they try to persuade a parent or adult to their point of view—that's when the sparks may fly. So let them know upfront that you're happy to hear their side of things, but that you have just as strong feelings as they do, no matter what they come up with.

One way to keep the volume level down at the household table is to avoid emotionally charged topics—those subjects that make a parent's face turn red and the neck veins stick out. Emotionally charged issues include curfew, dating, friends, clothes, hair, and music. All parents have strong opinions about certain matters. What fosters a combative atmosphere in the home is that parents argue, many times, against the peer group. For example, the daughter may say, "Amy's parents let her stay out past midnight."

At this point, the parent must argue principle and not argue against peer pressure. If the parent argues peer pressure, the parent loses. If thc parent argues principle, he or she has a sporting chance.

What is the principle behind not staying out late with Amy?

Don't things tend to deteriorate after midnight?

First Peter 3:15 says, "Always be prepared to give an answer to everyone who asks you to give the reason for the hope that you have. But do this with gentleness and respect." Notice two key words that describe the way the parent should respond: with *gentleness* and *respect*. Responding to argumentative teenagers on peer pressure questions is difficult. If the parent blows up and verbally rips them to shreds, the teen will be reluctant to bring up the subject again. Sadly, when this happens, teenagers take their questions elsewhere—to friends, schoolmates, teachers, or employers. But the parent needs to know who their teen's friends, schoolmates, teachers, and employers are.

One more point about arguing: pick your battles carefully. Don't make mountains out of molehills. While you want to help shape our teenagers' thinking, you don't want to drive them to exasperation. Ephesians 6:4 says, "Fathers, do not exasperate your children; instead, bring them up in the training and instruction of the Lord." *Exasperate* can mean to provoke, embitter, or irritate. There is nothing wrong with having strong feelings and opinions about some matters, and wise teenagers will stay away from those matters that stir up their parents. But when they begin to "push the envelope," parents need to decide if this is worth fighting over. Does it really matter how they wear their hair? Keep principle in mind. If it's principle, argue away. If it's not, lighten up. Remember, teenagers will have questions about many things. Do what you can to keep the communication lines open between you and them.

Teenagers must understand that a boundary may seem unreasonable or an issue may seem insignificant to them, but if it's a hot-button issue with their parents, teens need to obey their parents. The old adage "while you live under my roof" may not resonate with kids, but it still makes sense while they remain on their parents' "payroll." In the meantime, parents should pick their fights carefully and selectively. And those fights should be few and far between. Parents may have to yield some minor battles while they fight the critical ones. When it's a life-and-death matter, figuratively or realistically, then "fight the good fight," stand in the way, be a prude, be stubborn, old, and boring.

Imaginary Audience

Teenagers have an imaginary audience; they think they are always on stage. As a result, they are overly concerned about their appearance and behavior. Now you know why it takes teenagers so long to get ready. "Everyone" will be watching them, or so they think. Remember, they are beginning to think. So in their thinking processes, they think that everyone is concerned about them. Of course this isn't true, except in their own minds. This imaginary audience usually diminishes with age. As teenagers mature and celebrate birthdays, the imaginary audience becomes less and less a factor in their lives.

What are adults and parents to do? First of all, they need to be sensitive about teens' public exposure. This is something that needs to be avoided, or at least, parents should know how much their teenagers can handle.

Secondly, public criticism and ridicule should be avoided. There simply is no place for this when working or living among teenagers.

Thirdly, never point out physiological features, no matter how innocent this may seem. Don't put up with it on an occasion. Parents and adults must have a zero-tolerance policy. Don't remind a teenage girl that she has a complexion problem. She already knows. Don't remind a teenage guy that he is skinny. He already knows. Stating facts like this fractures any opportunity for a meaningful relationship with this teenager.

Finally, avoid labels. The problem with labels is that teenagers tend to live up or down to their labels. A teenage guy that's been called "dumb" or a "retard" just might live down to that label. A teenage girl who has been labeled "easy" or a "ho" just might live down to that label. Instead, give teenagers labels they can live up to—hard workers, sensitive, friendly, thoughtful, smart.

I had a teenager in my youth group whose name was A.L. He was one of those teenagers who didn't know he was goofy even though other kids were making fun of him. A.L. was frumpy, red-haired, and a bit outgoing. It was my practice to give equal attention to all my teenagers, and I gave special attention to A.L. He even tried to morph himself into me by cutting his hair the way I did. That's scary! Later, our family moved to Alberta, Canada, and I lost touch with A.L. Then one day A.L. called me. It had been almost ten years. Yet he talked to me as if I was still his youth pastor. He was a truck driver and had taken a job that would take him to Edmonton, Alberta where I live. This trip would be a "deadhead" trip (meaning he will go up fully loaded but come back empty). He probably wouldn't make any money on it, but he wanted to see me. So we connected at his drop-off location. When he stepped out of the eighteen-wheeler, I couldn't believe how big he was. A.L. was no longer a frumpy, non-athletic kid, but he was a muscular 6'8" man. We embraced and had a great weekend together. We talked about what had taken place in his life. When I last saw him, he was just going into high school. He had gotten bigger and stronger, and discovered a love for football. He started every game on the defensive line.

"I love hittin' people, Pastor Steve," he said with a grin.

Then after high school, he became a U.S. Army Ranger. During that time, the U.S. had a drug problem and particularly, a drug lord in Nicaragua named General Manuel Noriega, who was thumbing his nose at us. So in December of 1989, President Bush (#41) gave his okay to engage in Operation Just Cause, so the U.S. Army invaded and captured General Noriega. A.L. was one of the soldiers who helped capture him. As he was parachuting down at night, gunshots whizzed past, barely missing him.

"What'd you do?" I asked.

"I shot back. I liked shooting guns, Pastor Steve," he said with that familiar grin.

As I listened to his amazing story, I was in awe that this once-upon-a-time teenager in my youth group had made a blip on the "historical radar screen." You never know!

Self-centered

Everything that happens to them is unique and exclusive. They exclaim, "I can't believe this happened to me!" or "No one has it as tough as I do!" They don't realize that whatever has happened to them has happened to thousands or millions of others. And believe it or not, some teens on planet earth do have it tougher than they do.

Parents and youth workers need to show teenagers that they can learn volumes from other people's experiences. Introduce them to stories of those who have gone before, the experiences they faced, and the lessons they learned. Point out how other individuals are unique, just as they are unique.

Decision Making

Ever wonder why fast-food restaurants are so popular with teenagers? It's because teenagers have difficulty making decisions. They go to the counter (or drive-through) and order by numbers. The only thing they have to decide on is a number between one and ten and whether to place the order as super size or value size order. Take them to a restaurant where the menu is in cursive, and what do they look for? Burger and fries.

Okay, maybe this is a bit overstated, but what about picking out clothes? What they pick out may seem bizarre to most parents. But adults and parents need to keep in mind that the major difference between an adult and a teenager in the decision-making process is one word: experience. Not that adults are necessarily smarter than teenagers, but they certainly are more experienced. Teens need help in making decisions. Here are some questions for teens to consider before they make significant decisions:

- Is there a conflict or command in the Scripture about this matter?
- What do other people say about it, especially parents or friends who have your best interests at heart?
- Is the Holy Spirit giving you any leading and direction?
- What would help you the most spiritually?
- Do circumstances line up?
- Are there any negative, harmful, or irreversible consequences?
- Once you've made the decision, can you make it work?

A biblical example of a decision maker is Joshua, who made his decision explicitly clear: "Now fear the LORD and serve him with all faithfulness. Throw away the gods your forefathers worshiped beyond the River and in Egypt, and serve the Lord. But if serving the Lord seems undesirable to you, then choose for yourselves this day whom you will serve, whether the gods your forefathers served beyond the River, or the gods of the Amorites, in whose land you are living. But as for me and my household, we will serve the Lord" (Josh. 24:14–15).

Have you noticed that teenagers are quick to mouth off? They vocalize the way they see things without any consideration of personal involvement. There's a lot more talk than walk. One day as I was walking on a high-school campus, I met a student who had a "Save the Whales" button on her jacket.

"What have you done to save the whales?" I asked.

"I bought this button!" she said.

Wow, talk about involvement!

So how can adults help teenagers? They must find ways to get teenagers involved in meaningful work. Talk with them about serving others, going to the mission field, or doing evangelism. The next step would be the application of these subjects. Look around. I'm sure there are service opportunities staring them in the face. Take teens on a mission trip. Make it an arduous experience, one they will never forget. Or plan an evangelistic event that your teenagers can get excited about. Provide walk with the talk.

Spiritually

The fact that God is a personal God is appealing to young people. But here's the catch, teenagers must move from parental faith to personal faith. I would never want to minimize the faith of parents influencing their teenagers.

Parental faith gives teenagers the opportunity to commit to a personal faith. While parents are anxious about their teenagers' faith, the young people themselves must make it their own personal faith.

Is there anything else?

Overwhelmed? Don't be. All parents of teenagers go through the trials of trying to understand what is happening to their teen and how to deal with them. Honestly, I was nervous when my three kids approached their teen years. Being a youth pastor, would I do a good job to parent my own teenagers? Now that my kids have moved through their teens, I can honestly say that I enjoyed those years. Did we get it right all the time? No. But it's nice to look back and see that my kids didn't mind being around dear old dad and mom. We included them in as much as we could. We got involved in their lives. We helped them pursue their dreams. We got on them when they messed up. The irony in parenting is that you don't become an expert until your kids are grown. From this vantage point, I can look back and see what my wife and I could have done better—along with what worked and what didn't.

The teenage years are only seven years long (give or take a year or two due to various maturation levels). These years are pivotal in the morphing of a teenager into a responsible adult. So you need to take advantage of the time you have. It's shorter than you think.

chapter 2

Mandate

This book was born out of a desire to see today's youth obey the Word of God while living in a culture that is set against them. It will take extreme obedience if they are to survive. There's a gap between what kids say they believe and how they actually live their lives. Headline stories and news programs illustrate scenes of despair in today's current youth culture.

Recently, a survey was completed concerning the moral standards of today's youth—both believers and nonbelievers. The survey found there was only a 4 percent difference between the two groups. Let's suppose the survey question was: "Have you lied to your parents in the past month?" Seventy percent of the non-Christian kids would have answered yes, while the Christian kids would have said yes, 66 percent of the time. This 4 percent difference was true in every category. This tells us that there is virtually no difference in the moral standards between Christian and non-Christian youth.

What are parents and adults to do? They cannot sit back and watch their teens make bad decisions and develop the same moral standards as their unsaved friends. It's the parents' and Christian leaders' responsibility to help their teens live lives of conviction. The biblical mandate to live in obedience is for all believers, regardless of age. Training one's kids to be persons of conviction is the greatest responsibility that parents and youth workers have. Teens need to learn to stand on the principles of Scripture regardless of the situation.

As you read the following chapters of this book, remember we're talking about obedience to God, not simply having good manners toward others. Your quest starts with Scripture.

Our Marching Orders

The Scriptures listed here are not intended to be an exhaustive list of verses that speak on the topic of living lives of conviction. Our purpose is to formulate enough Scripture to gain an understanding of what we'll be talking about throughout the book and to help you understand the progression that should be followed as you train your teens to live in extreme obedience to God. Each area that is touched upon will be covered in more depth in later chapters. The following verses are foundational to all further discussion.

First, our whole heart has to be committed to living a life of obedience; this is a requirement if you're to be successful. We will not succeed if you do anything half-baked. "The LORD thy God commands you this day to follow these decrees and laws; carefully observe them with all your heart and with all your soul" (Deut. 26:16).

Second, we must put effort into our spiritual growth if we're to be successful. It will not happen by accident or by chance. At some point, we must decide to spend time reading the Word of God so we can learn and understand what it is that God would have us do. "Do not let this Book of the Law depart from your mouth; meditate on it therein day and night, so you that may be careful to do everything written in it. Then you will be prosperous and successful" (Josh. 1:8).

Third, Scripture clearly shows how conviction plays out in our life and the choices we must make to obey those convictions. "But Samuel replied: Does the LORD delight in burnt offerings and sacrifices as much as in obeying the voice of the LORD? To obey is better than sacrifice, and to heed is better than the fat of rams" (1 Sam. 15:22).

Fourth, obedience secures our entrance into heaven. "Not everyone who says to me, Lord, Lord, will enter the kingdom of heaven, but only he who does the will of my Father who is in heaven" (Matthew 7:21, KJV).

Fifth, our duty is to bring glory to God through obedience to him. "This is to my Father's glory, that you bear much fruit, showing yourselves to be my disciples" (John 15:8). "Peter and the other apostles replied: 'we must obey God rather than men!'" (Acts 5:29).

Finally, Jesus' own words concerning obedience points to the importance of following God. Jesus stated that obedience is the foundation of character: "Therefore everyone who hears these words of mine and puts them into practice is like a wise man who built his house on the rock," (Matt. 7:24). Obedience is also the proof of our membership in the family of God: "For whoever does the will of my Father in heaven is my brother and sister and mother" (Matt. 12:50). Obedience is the key to spiritual knowledge: "If anyone chooses to do God's will, he will find out whether my teaching comes from God or whether I speak on my own," (John 7:17), and the basis of our fellowship with Him: "If anyone loves me, he will obey my teaching. My father will love him, and we will come to him and make our home with him," (John 14:23).

The orders are clear: obedience to the Word of God is not something we should consider lightly. We should involve our whole hearts, our time, and our efforts as we seek to bring glory to God. How do parents accomplish this in the lives of our teens? By becoming people of conviction, which comes by maintaining proper mindsets.

The Process

From these verses, parents can see that they need to obey God to grow spiritually into people of conviction. This is also the case for their kids. It involves three aspects.

First, becoming persons of conviction is a developmental process. *Developmental* means "to bring, grow, or evolve to a more complete, complex, or desirable state." In other words, it takes time and effort to become a person of conviction. It will not happen overnight just because teens go to church or live under the same roof as parents who have a relationship with God. Of course, these things help; however, they aren't a guarantee that your teens will live by the principles of Scripture. Someone has said, "God has no grandchildren." Your kids have to claim their faith as their own. They need to understand and know what they believe and why they believe it.

This process can be likened to growing and maturing physically. When a child is born, he doesn't come out of the womb ready to run a one-hundred-yard dash or even a ten-yard-dash, for that matter. The process is quite the opposite. He must first gain the strength to hold his head up by himself. The next step is to sit up, then crawl, then walk, and finally run. During the process, he will fall over again and again, only to pick himself up and try over and over until he succeeds. He didn't quit until he was walking and then running. The process of being able to run physically starts with baby steps.

We expect our kids to run as Christians when we haven't even trained them to crawl. We expect them to take leaps and bounds when they need to take baby steps. We may expect spiritual maturity out of our kids when they are not capable of delivering. We can't skip a step physically, and we can't skip a step spiritually. It takes time. As we help them take baby steps, they one day will run.

Second, we need to feed teenagers appropriate spiritual food. New babies cannot handle T-bone steaks. They must be fed food they can digest and that their systems can handle. It takes proper physical food to grow and become strong. It's the same when it comes to spiritual food. We cannot serve them spiritual steak if they need mashed-up peas. The food must be something they can digest so they can grow and mature spiritually. We have to make sure that the spiritual food is edible, or they will reject it.

Third, remember that teens mature at different rates. Some mature quickly while others mature slowly. It's the same way spiritually. Some young people understand spiritual truths and apply them to their lives with no problem. Others struggle with the same spiritual truths and have trouble applying them. Bottom line: Teens develop spiritually at different rates but hopefully they will continue to progress.

The Progression

"And Jesus grew in wisdom and stature, and in favor with God and men" (Luke 2:52).

Even though becoming persons of conviction is a developmental process, we should see progression in our teens, regardless of how fast or how slow the pace. As long as they are moving forward spiritually, they are going in the right direction. They should progress based on their own abilities. The goal we're striving for is *obedience*.

Consider these truths in Hebrews: "In fact, though by this time you ought to be teachers, you need someone to teach you the elementary truths of God's word all over again. You need milk, not solid food!" (Heb. 5:12) What is the writer saying here? Simply that these believers should have been feeding on the meat of the Word, but they were still drinking milk. Spiritually, they were not progressing in their spiritual understanding or in their obedience to God. The writer rebukes them for their lack of making progress spiritually; in fact, he suggests they go back to the basics and learn them again.

Sometimes we think that the number of years we've been Christians or the amount of time we spend in church has something to do with our spiritual progress. Outside of obedience it doesn't. So the question becomes: How can we tell if our teens' spiritual lives are progressing? Use the following verses as guidelines to show whether or not our kids are moving in the right spiritual direction:

> The acts of the sinful nature are obvious: sexual immorality, impurity and debauchery; idolatry and witchcraft; hatred, discord, jealousy, fits of rage, selfish ambition, dissensions, factions and envy; drunkenness, orgies, and the like. I warn you, as I did before, that those who live like this will not inherit the kingdom of God. But the fruit of the Spirit is love, joy, peace, patience, kindness, goodness, faithfulness, gentleness and self-control. Against such things there is no law (Gal. 5:19–23).

As you read and think through these verses, be honest with yourself as well as with your teens. You must see things for what they are. To gloss over problems or situations will not benefit anyone. To shrug them off might bring temporary peace to the family; however, your teens will be in worse conditions if you ignore behavior that is contrary to Scripture.

As parents, youth workers, and concerned adults, you have marching orders to train and equip your teens to obey scriptural principles. You need to see this as a developmental process, understanding that it will take time and effort for both you and your teens.

Finally, progress must be made. Your kids' lives should be different from the world. You can help raise a generation of youth that follow God with extreme obedience! The following chapters will help you achieve this goal.

"Whoever claims to live in him must walk as Jesus did" (1 John 2:6).

chapter 3

Conviction

Let's suppose you're sick. You drag yourself to the doctor's office and sit in a waiting room for thirty to forty minutes with all the others who feel the same as you do. It's hot, and the only thing to read is a six-month old *Sports Illustrated*. The nurse finally calls your name. Now you sit in a small examination room where you wait for another thirty to forty minutes with no reading material. The doctor comes in, examines you for ten minutes, and charges you seventy dollars. He gives you a prescription, which will cost you another fifty to seventy-five dollars and twenty minutes to get it filled. After almost two hours of your time and one hundred plus dollars later, you decide not to take the prescribed pills.

Let's say you have a personal problem. You seek advice from someone you respect or at least feel can give wisdom, insight, and possible solutions. You listen to what this wise person says, but you ignore the advice. Then you ask others the same questions. You listen to what they have to say but never put their suggestions into practice.

Both examples are silly and stupid. Why go to the doctor to get a prescription to help you feel better and then never take it? Why seek wisdom from others about the issues you face, only to ignore their advice? It just doesn't make sense. In the same way, why go to church services, read God's Word, and pray only to ignore the direction God lays on our hearts through conviction? Why go through the motions and never apply the prescribed solutions?

The purpose of this chapter is to help your teens understand the role that convictions play in their lives and their need to obey those convictions. Conviction is God's prescription for what ails teens. God's prescription points out behaviors that should be changed. What happens if you ignore and depend on others to help your kids in this area?

Jimmy is an eighteen-year-old believer, a freshman in college. He's away from home, his youth group, and his church for the first time in his life. He has no one on a day-to-day basis telling him what's right and what's wrong. His circle of influence that he depended on over the past few years is gone. Jimmy attended church his whole life and was a leader in his youth group.

Jimmy, however, has a problem. No one taught him how to obey convictions that come from Scripture. Although his parents and youth leaders encouraged him to read and be in God's Word, they did not teach him how to make his faith real by obeying Scripture. Now he's thrust into an environment that demands he makes biblically correct choices on his own. Will he succeed? The odds are he will not.

Statistics show that the church loses most of its youth during the college years due to the lack of helping kids develop their own faith through obedience to Scripture. In fact, recent studies show that they are not coming back.

There's a "Jimmy" who sits in my classes every semester. He's a good kid, a smart kid, a kid with all the potential in the world. However, he struggles with living his faith in a way that displays Christ to those around him because he's not obeying scriptural principles. Maybe his downfall is alcohol, girls, or other bad choices that leave him struggling. He's not growing in his relationship with the Lord, so he's frustrated, and stops trying to live a Christian life. He's not a bad kid, but he's not obedient either. Some would say he's "playing the game" well.

As I deal with the "Jimmys" of the world, I am amazed that our youth are not being told how to live the convictions that come from obeying the Word of God. And as I talk to and listen to parents of teens, this issue gets little if any attention. Maybe Mom and Dad feel secure because their teens, like Jimmy, are involved in the church and are just good kids. Or they may rely on the youth pastor or programs of the church to take this responsibility.

As believers we all experience Holy Spirit convictions, either from Scripture or decisions we make. When a Bible verse hits home or when we do something we know is wrong, we're convicted. However, as we experience these convictions, we have a choice to either ignore them or obey them.

Make no mistake, Scripture is clear as to which way we should go:

- "This is love for God: to obey his commands" (1 John 5:3).
- "Put off your old self . . . and to put on the new self, created to be like God in true righteousness and holiness" (Eph. 4:22, 24).
- "Do not merely listen to the word, and so deceive yourselves. Do what it says. Anyone who listens to the word but does not do

> what it says is like a man who looks at his face in the mirror and, after looking at himself, goes away and immediately forgets what he looks like. But the man who looks intently into the perfect law that gives freedom, and continues to do this, not forgetting what he has heard, but doing it he will be blessed in what he does" (James 1:22–25).

The command is clear: we need to help our teens live lives of conviction.

Before we get to the specifics of helping teens to understand and obey when convicted, we need to define the terms used in this chapter as well as those that follow. Conviction, surrender, service, and obedience mean different things but are knit together and depend on each other. Each one succeeds by leaning on the others. Don't think "to-do list" but think "spider web" where each strand is interwoven with the rest. If one strand is broken or weak, the web is less effective.

Conviction + Surrender + Service = Obedience

For our purposes, let's use the following definitions:

Conviction: A Holy Spirit prompting within that lets a person know that some action, attitude, or behavior needs to be corrected. This comes from Scripture as well as feedback from our actions and attitudes.

Surrender: It means to yield to the power of another. It's giving into God's desire for our actions in contrast to giving into our own sinful desires. An attitude of thinking: "God whatever you ask, I will do."

Service: It is living out the above terms in all situations.

Obedience: It is the action of understanding and following the Holy Spirit's prompting.

Let's look at conviction and the role it plays in leading teens to conform to the image of Christ. Conviction (non-spiritual) can be defined as a fixed or strong belief. Sounds simple enough, but the fixed or strong belief must be acted on. Otherwise, it's just a feeling or a realization that something must be changed. For example, I may realize that I need to spend more time praying for and with my kids. However, unless I act on that realization, that's all it is—simply a realization that I should change an aspect of my life. A strong or fixed belief should move me to act on it, to incorporate it, and change my life based on the realization or conviction.

Abraham Lincoln said, "I have been driven many times to my knees by the overwhelming conviction that I had nowhere else to go." That strong belief resulted in action. Conviction without action is like a car without gas. It's useless.

How does that relate to our teens? A by-product of reading God's Word regularly is conviction. It's part of the Holy Spirit's ministry in the life of the believer. So as we read the Bible, conviction will follow. I read that "each of you should look not only to your own interests, but also to the interests of others" (Phil. 2:4). That verse hits hard, and I experience conviction, a realization that I need to pay attention to the needs of those around me. What are my options at this point?

1. I could acknowledge the conviction, quietly nod my head in agreement, and say to myself: *I need to do a better job at this.* I close my Bible and never attempt to change. This is disobedience.
2. Or I could ignore the conviction and continue on my way. That again is disobedience.
3. Or I could say to myself: *Yes, I need to fix this area of my life* and obey the conviction.

When our teens make a commitment to obey the conviction, they are moving into surrender. Remember, surrender is a willingness, no matter the cost, to do anything at any time for God. Where do we go from here?

First, we must help our teens realize that conviction is a good thing. It comes from God and is one of his ways to help us glorify him in our lives. Many teens confuse conviction with guilt. They are not the same thing. Nonbelievers experience guilt, as they do not have the ministry of the Holy Spirit in their lives. Believers experience conviction. They might mistake conviction for guilt about certain actions, attitudes, behaviors, or from fear of getting caught, or what others might think of them. The conviction that they could have handled situations differently or obeyed the rules, is a good thing. It's one way of God's protecting them.

My own teens, from time to time, bend the rules. When my wife or I confront them, asking why they did what they knew they shouldn't do, sometimes they reply, "I don't know; I just wanted to." As frustrating as this is, it's a great chance remind them that if they can't obey our rules now, they'll have a tough time obeying God when they are on their own. Teens need to understand that no one is perfect, and we all fail. But God promises us, "If we confess our sins, he is faithful and just and will forgive us our sins and purify us from all unrighteousness," (1 John 1:9). However, this is not an excuse to continue in behavior that we've been convicted about.

In addition, conviction when acted upon accomplishes the following:

- We gain more responsibility. Jesus said, "Whoever can be trusted with very little can also be trusted with much" (Luke 16:10).

- Doors of service will open up. Paul said, "A great door for effective work has opened to me" (1 Cor. 16:9).
- We enjoy fellowship with God and others. John wrote, "If we walk in the light, as he [God] is in the light, we have fellowship with one another" (1 John 1:7).
- Obedience is the cornerstone of our character. Jesus said, "Therefore everyone who hears these words of mine and puts them into practice is like a wise man who built his house on the rock" (Matt. 7:24).
- Obedience is also the key to spiritual understanding. Jesus said, "If anyone chooses to do God's will, he will find out whether my teaching comes from God or whether I speak on my own" (John 7:17).

Second, we must help our teens understand that conviction isn't determined by the length of time that they've been believers, or the amount of time they spend in church on a weekly basis. It's about obedience and their surrender to God's will.

Third, we must help our teens understand that *should*, *could*, *ought*, and *must* are not the same as *will*. If they stop at the acknowledgment stage they are in danger of not being convicted of that sin any longer. In fact this can hamper the Spirit's ministry in their lives. As James reminds us, if we hear the Word and ignore it, we deceive ourselves (see James 1:27). Simply put, most of us think we're more spiritual than we really are. Teens may attend youth groups, Bible studies, Young Life, other meetings. They may read the Word, pray, and memorize Scripture. All of these are good things, but if they are done without putting conviction into action, they are pointless. This means we must help our teens know themselves, their weaknesses, their areas of temptation, as well as the places and people that might hamper them from living with conviction.

Fourth, we must help teens formulate a "game plan" to carry out obedience to the conviction by stating "I will . . . (be as specific as you can)." Have them write these plans down. When a person writes goals down on paper, he or she has a greater likelihood to sticking to them.

The only limit here is—how deep is the desire to obey?

An "I will" statement might read something like this:

- "I will make an effort to consider other people's needs." Not bad. Now ask the teen how he will consider others' needs.
- He may write, "I will pray each day that God makes me sensitive to others' needs." Better. This is more specific then the first.

Keep going until specific plans of action are down on paper. Be patient. Help instruct each of your teens to formulating game plans they can live with. The goal is to help them now so when they are on their own and out of your direct influence, they will continue to own their faith and have lifelong convictions.

Fifth, we must help our teens "work the plan," that is, put their "I will" statements into practice. Without action such statements are pointless. Now help them evaluate their progress. Get them to thinking about proper choices before they are confronted with them. Encourage them to get specific in regard to living out their faith in obedience to the Word of God.

Remember "Jimmy?" He talks with me about the struggles he's facing. He feels that something isn't right; he's lost the desire to serve God and utilize his gifts. He can't understand it. He grew up in the church and has been a believer for a long time. He's even reading the Bible on a consistent basis, however, something is missing. Something is not right, but he can't put his finger on it.

Jimmy and I begin by talking about his Christian walk and his obedience to the things God is laying on his heart. Bingo! We find the problem. When Jimmy is convicted, he is not obeying the convictions. He's lacking obedience, surrender, and service. We talk about why God has commanded us to obey his Word and not simply listen to it.

As your teens read the Bible, whether in their own quiet times or in a Bible study, have them also pray, asking God to reveal the following to them:

1. "Be perfect, therefore, as your heavenly Father is perfect" (Matt. 5:48). *Perfect* here means mature or complete growth in their mental and moral aspects. What life changes need to take place? What areas of their thoughts and morals need to align more with being like Christ?
2. "Do you not know that your body is a temple of the Holy Spirit, who is in you, whom you have received from God? You are not your own; you were bought at a price. Therefore honor God with your body" (1 Cor. 6:19, 20). Based on this passage, have your teens ask God to reveal to them areas concerning stewardship (the idea that they're managers of someone else's property). Their time, talents, and treasure all belong to him. How can they glorify Christ through their lives?

3. "You will receive power when the Holy Spirit comes on you; and you will be my witnesses in Jerusalem, and in all Judea and Samaria, and to the ends of the earth" (Acts 1:8). Ask your teens about their personal testimonies, not how they became saved but their lifestyles. What areas need changing to make them better witnesses?
4. As they read their Bibles, they should look for solutions to their individual questions. This dependence on God's divine wisdom and desire for their lives develops personal faith, one that they own for themselves—not yours, not the pastors, and not the youth pastors' faith. This will help them survive as adults in today's culture.

If your teens ask God to reveal these areas to them, you'd better believe that he will. So what can you do? First, talk with your teens about their Bible reading and what God is putting on their hearts. Ask questions like:

- What have you learned this week from Scripture?
- Do you have questions about what you've discovered?
- What can I do to help you live like a Christian in a non-Christian world?
- What can you do? How will you do it?

This will help them understand how to respond to conviction. Do not leave this up to someone else. Now they have to surrender to God's will and be obedient, no matter what.

My son plays baseball. It's in his blood. After every game, I ask him one question: "Parker, did you try your best today?" If the response is no (which isn't very often), I ask, "Why not?" To this day he has never had a good excuse as to why he didn't try his best. If he's not feeling well, has an injury, or just doesn't feel like playing, he has learned that no matter the circumstance, he needs to play each game at his best.

That's a great example of how our teens will have to give an answer to God some day. When God asks them if they were obedient, regardless of the circumstances, what excuses will he accept? "I was tired." "Peer pressure made me do it." "I really wanted to." "I know it was wrong, but it looked like fun." These excuses will not cut it. I can hear God say, "Those are good excuses; however, I asked you to accomplish something, to behave differently, and gave you the power to succeed." They really have no reason not to obey.

The tough part for teens is that the decision to obey or not is theirs. You can't continue to do it for them. Recently, a student came to me for help with his spiritual growth. We talked about where he was spiritually, and I made the above suggestions. The following week when we got together to discuss his "I will" statements and how he was implementing them, he said, "I just can't make the commitment to change. It's too hard. What if I fail?"

What would you have said? Think about it, because as you work with your teens, you'll hear the same type of excuses. Surrendering to God is not easy and it has its costs. For our kids, it could be popularity, friends, boyfriends or girlfriends, and in some cases broken or strained family relationships. The world today is not the same for teens as it was when the parents were teens. The cards are stacked against them. The question, however, remains: How bad do they want to obey? Will it be Christ or culture? It really is a question of authority. Will they follow their God-given convictions or will they give in to their sinful desires? They can't have it both ways.

At this point, the difference is civility versus surrender. Civility is simply being civil with good manners and the expected behavior of society. Surrender is giving up our rights and following what God has laid on our hearts. Most of our teens know how to play the game. They are civil, good kids like "Jimmy." However, the issue here is producing teens that stand for what is right because surrendering to God and God alone is the right thing to do.

The key to helping our teens live lives of conviction is accountability. This will be described in the following chapter.

chapter 4

Accountability

Raising kids in today's culture is not easy; it's difficult and often times frustrating. However, as parents, you have to hold your ground. One big mistake parents make is that they're afraid that if they hold their teens to consequences that they will not be their friends when they grow up. This "objective" affects every decision they make. If this is your motivation, let me urge you to change your thought process now. If you want to be friends with your teens as they grow older, aim to produce better Christians then you ever were. But if fear motivates you, then you've lost already. As accountability and consequences are discussed, you have to decide to play the parent no matter how loud it gets or how quiet it becomes. You will have to be strong and stand your ground.

This chapter will discuss accountability for obedience to convictions, provide some examples, and discuss the consequences.

Accountability

Simply stated, accountability is holding someone answerable, to give an explanation for a behavior or a decision that has been made. You must hold your teens accountable to obey the convictions that have been placed on their hearts. They should be able to explain their behaviors and the decisions they have made. Too often, parents and youth workers never follow up on the choices that teens make. They assume that because they've talked about how to live like Christians that they're living that way. This simply is not the case (see our book *Disturbing Behaviors*). Parents must follow up, ask hard questions, and get involved in the lives of their teens. Conviction and the obedience to that conviction will not happen without accountability. Remind your teens that some sort of accountability is all around us. The police hold us accountable to obey the law, teachers hold students accountable for their work through tests, papers, and grades. And one day we all will answer to God. As Paul said, "So then, each of us will give an account of himself to God" (Rom. 14:12). Accountability is a necessary and good thing. Don't feel as if you're invading their privacy. Ask questions.

How do you hold your teens accountable? What methods can you utilize? This is where the "I will . . ." statements discussed in the previous chapter come into play. By having your teens write down these specific statements, they are giving you a measuring stick with which to hold them accountable. Utilize their statements as starting points to ask questions concerning their obedience to those specific areas of life change. As you talk with your teens, keep in mind that these are their instructions to themselves. You've not asked them to do these things, but they are their own personal convictions. They wrote them, so it's up to them to live them. If you remind them of that, it will not seem as if you're demanding specific behaviors from them but simply following up on actions, attitudes, and behaviors that they came up with. Remember that you cannot think for them in every situation. However, you can equip them to make proper choices and to think biblically.

Second, adjust, revise, and evaluate the statements as needed. Adults can state behavioral goals that are over their heads. Some reworking might need to be done. Be patient, understanding, and listen to your teens as they work through this. Give guidance as needed. The only boundary here is that you do not let them justify disobedience. Their "I will" statements may be right on, but they lack the effort that comes from complete surrender to the conviction. How can you tell? Pray! Don't forget this important aspect. Ask God to give you wisdom and insight as you work with your teens.

As your teens succeed and fail in living lives of extreme obedience, you'll want to handle each success and failure differently. Let's say that your daughter has been reading Scripture, and she gets convicted about her thought life. She takes the next step and comes up with an "I will" statement that is specific and doable. She examines all the media that she is exposed to—the Internet, television, books, movies, magazines, and video games—to determine what boundaries need to be established. If any one thing is influencing her in the wrong direction, she is determined not to view it, to read it, or to play it. Now, she will either succeed or fail in living according to the conviction. It's up to her, but you can hold her accountable to her action plan because she has given you guidelines to follow.

As teens succeed in living out their convictions, you'll want to do the following:

1. *Encourage.* One success doesn't guarantee continued success. Make sure that you encourage your teens to surrender to God and follow through on their action plans.

2. *Reinforce.* Go through the steps, the thought processes they had as they made the decisions to obey. Have them write these down so they remember them the next time.
3. *Celebrate.* Do something special, take them out for dinner, or give rewards to celebrate their obedience. They have experienced convictions, surrendered to them, and have lived out their action plans. In short, they've been obedient to God; they've done the right thing. Doesn't this deserve a ho-ho? Celebrate!

If they fail:

1. *Encourage correct behavior.* Talk through the reasons again of why they wrote down the "I will" statements in the first place. Remind them of the blessings that come from obedience to God's desires (as listed in the previous chapter).
2. *How to do it differently.* Think through ways they could have handled situations differently. That way if they ever find themselves faced with choices to obey or not, they'll be better equipped to succeed. As always, have them write it down. This list will help you with accountability if it happens again.
3. *Consequences.* These will be discussed later in the chapter.
4. *Childishness versus foolishness.* Scriptures list these two kinds of behaviors. The difference? Childishness does not know better,

while foolishness knows better but does it anyway. Let me explain: When I was growing up, my parents had a rule that my brother and I should not wrestle at the top of the stairs. If we did wrestle at the top of the stairs before we knew the rule, that was childishness. If we wrestled at the top of the stairs after we knew the rule that was foolishness. We had no excuse; we knew the rule but chose to disobey. Scripture is clear that foolishness is not acceptable.

5. *Unconditional love.* No matter how much you're hurt or discouraged, don't let anything come between you and your teens. You don't have to agree, in fact you don't have to be happy, but you have to love. Anything less will push them in the other direction.

The key is to ask questions. This may be a shock to their systems, especially if you've never done this before. But stay encouraged and stand your ground as you seek to help your teen live a life of conviction. It's never too late to put this into practice.

Consequences

Consequences fall into two categories: natural and imposed. A natural consequence happens naturally. When my brother and I wrestled at the top of the stairs, possible natural consequences could be that we tumbled down the stairs, getting bumps, bruises, or broken bones. If we had tumbled down the stairs, we would have learned not to do that again. It would have cost us something, not to mention possible medical costs, new furniture, and time.

Natural consequences can also be found in the spiritual realm as well. If we knowingly sin, Scripture tells us that we will experience misery (see Rom. 2:9), spiritual and physical death (see Rom. 5:12), and separation from God (see Isa. 59:2). The bottom line is that each decision we make carries with it a set of natural consequences. Sometimes these alone are enough to bring about the desired behavior. Sometimes they are not, especially from a spiritual standpoint. The spiritual consequences may be delayed and not immediately recognized or felt. Nonetheless, they are present. This means that you, as a parent, may have to impose consequences in addition to the natural ones.

Imposed consequences are the penalties you lay down when expected behavior is not achieved. Each teen is different, and each situation has a different set of circumstances surrounding it. Consequences you establish in one situation might not hold up in others or might work with different kids. You can be creative here. Think about which imposed consequences will best impact your teens.

Reconsider the example of your daughter and her thought life. If she decides she will only go to appropriate Websites and fails, then a consequence needs to be imposed. Maybe it's the loss of the Internet for a week or two. You may need to install a firewall program that will block certain types of Websites. No instant messaging for a time. Whatever you decide needs to be stated up front and then stuck to. No going back on the consequences that you've imposed for not sticking to the rules.

Most parents fail when it comes to this area with their teens. They seldom talk through expected behavior, and if they do, they don't talk about the resulting consequences. In fact, they bribe instead of communicate. I'm sure you've overheard conversations between mom and child in a grocery store:

"If you just behave so I can get my shopping done, I'll buy you a candy bar or a treat on the way out."

What is that instilling in young children about obedience? And as they mature, they continue to learn how to "play the game" by being civil. Parents offer the same thing with their teens:

"If you clean your room, then you can play the X-box."

Instead you should exchange a few words about expected behavior before the situation arises. Parents should communicate to their children how they need to behave before they enter into stores or communicate responsibilities about cleaning their rooms. Then set consequences if that behavior is not followed through. If parents decide to buy candy or allow the use of the X-box, it's to celebrate obedience, not to bribe.

God operates the same way with us and our teens. He communicates expected behavior through his Word. The specific things that we need to work on are pointed out to us through conviction. We make action plans and surrender to God's desires, then it's up to us to live it. God doesn't bribe us to live as we should. But he does equip us with the power and the will to do so. Your teens need to learn to do the right thing because it's the right thing to do.

As you hold your teens to consequences, I guarantee you'll hear the following: "You haven't forgiven me if there are still consequences." Most kids confuse forgiveness with consequences; they are not the same thing. They think that if you've forgiven them, then you will remove the consequences. One day I talked with a youth pastor who was struggling with a situation in his church. The worship leader for the youth ministry praise band had gotten his girlfriend pregnant. He was truly repentant and asked God and the youth group for forgiveness. He also asked how he should handle the situation as a young Christian. The struggle came when the youth pastor removed him from leading the worship team. The young man felt that since he had been forgiven, he only needed to deal with the natural consequences of his mistake. He had confused forgiveness with consequences. He said, "You don't love me because you removed me from the leadership position." I encouraged the youth pastor to stand firm and tell the teen that because he did love him, he was holding him to the consequences of his behavior. You will hear the same thing. The situation might not be as extreme as the above, but you will have to deal with this as you work with your teens.

Let me encourage you to maintain your stand, communicate to your teens the consequences of their behavior, and use discernment. Above all, be strong parents or youth workers.

chapter 5

Boundaries

The cruel irony in being a parent is that you become an expert in parenting about the same time that you become an empty nester. At this writing, I am on the precipice of that "nest" with two having flown away, and the one left is beginning to flap his wings. Not being an expert yet, we have a lot to worry about. We have safety issues with this post-9/11 world. Kidnappers snatch children. Sexual predators lurk everywhere, online as well as in our neighborhoods. Add to that the uncertainty of a terrorist-infested world.

Here's the quandary: Many experts are giving advice. Dr. Frank Furedi in his book *Paranoid Parenting* explains that parents have been so inundated by advice from experts that they no longer believe they are competent to raise their own kids. The only clear message parents get today from magazines, books, and talk shows is that they can't trust themselves. Parenting is too important to be left to parents, they say, so experts must fill the gap. Judith Harris claims that this paranoia has an effect on the parents who fall victim to it. She says, "Child rearing is robbed of the spontaneity and joy nature intended it to have. Parenting is a very anxious-ridden occupation nowadays."[1] It's as if we parents don't have a clue! So I am not trying to convince you that I'm right and you're wrong. Frankly, my expertise is a compilation of misgivings, mistakes, and impromptu decision making. And the jury is still out as to whether I was a good parent. Most of the time, parenting skills are a blend of philosophy, personal biases, and a teenager's idiosyncrasies. What works for one teen may not work on another. For some kids, all it takes is a look, and they melt into submission. For others, a "two by four" gets the job done (okay, a bit of an exaggeration). Yet along the way, I think I've gathered some helpful insights that might help with your journey of raising your teenagers.

Two Types of Boundaries

There are two types of boundaries: those that are not up for compromise (absolute) and those that develop as situations arise. For example, an absolute boundary would be stating to your teens that when it comes to the Internet, there is no privacy, period. No ifs, and, or buts. Their continued use of instant messaging, e-mail, and Web surfing depends totally on this boundary being followed. I know that if your teens have had unlimited, unsupervised access to the World Wide Web, implementing this boundary will be a struggle. You'll hear the words, "You don't trust me."

Two things to keep in mind: First, you would not lock your teens in their rooms with the Playboy Channel wired to their televisions. Yet the Web has far more dangers to offer. In fact, John Young of Teen Hopeline and ZJAM ministries told me, "Unsupervised Internet usage is more dangerous than alcohol in the life of a teen." When I heard him say this,

I thought he exaggerated. Yet as I work with teens and students, I believe this statement to be 100 percent correct.

Second, total trust is earned, not a right. My dad used to say, "You don't get all of my trust and a chance to lose it. You get some of my trust and a chance to gain more." At times, we, as parents, get scared, thinking that if we implement absolute boundaries with our kids, we'll lose them. Or we think that it's not worth the fight. Let me encourage you that you need to be the parent and do what's right because it's the right thing to do.

Situational boundaries are just that: The situation dictates what or how you'll help your teens respond to the problems at hand. Let's say that you know that your teens are struggling with their thought lives. The Holy Spirit has convicted them, and they know they need to respond. A boundary here might be no sexually charged movies, music, or video games. Anything that might tempt them is off-limits. At this point, it becomes: how much do they want to obey? Remember that recovering alcoholics don't go to happy hour for hot wings. They remove themselves totally from all temptations to drink.

A few years ago, the Cleveland Indians won the American League pennant while playing in Seattle. During the postgame celebration, a reporter saw Dennis Martinez run from the locker room when the champagne flowed. He followed him and asked,

"Dennis, where are you going? Your team just achieved its goal, the very thing that you play 162 games for, that you've trained your whole life for. You've won the American League pennant and are going to the World Series! Why aren't you in there with your team?"

"You don't understand. I'm a recovering alcoholic. If one drop of that champagne hits my lips, I'm done. I can't risk it!" Martinez responded, shocking the reporter.

Dennis Martinez had it right. If he wanted to stay sober, he knew he had to stick to his boundaries. It's the same for our teens.

Matters To Consider When Establishing Boundaries

Establishing boundaries gets a little tricky. How much is too much? How much is not enough? Boundaries should be appropriate for various ages. For instance, middle-school teens should not drive vehicles, while no young person should do drugs. So age needs to be taken into consideration. This is always challenged when parents are in a household that has kids in both groups.

The issue of exposure to adult subject matter needs to be considered as well. Today's culture has had a paradigm shift from sheltering the young to exposing them to all types of suggestive subject matter. They mistakenly think this will prepare society's offspring for life. My challenge to that type of thinking is capsulated in these verses: "For it is shameful even to mention what the disobedient do in secret" (Eph. 5:12). "But I want you to be wise about what is good, and innocent about what is evil" (Rom. 16:19). When you waste time watching some talk shows, you wonder how people can be so unashamed about their behaviors.

Boundaries should also be set for serious matters. Do you need to micromanage your teenagers as to how they clean their rooms or cut the grass? I suggest you show them how you want it done or how it should look.

My youngest son was proud that he had cut our lawn in record time, but it looked like overgrown rental property. So I explained what I wanted the yard to look like. To get it that way, he had to slow the lawnmower down, not cut it like a NASCAR driver trying to hold on to first place.

Beyond their rooms or yard work, consider how serious the matter is. You can judge seriousness by the degree of irreversible consequences. In other words, if mistakes are made resulting from poor decisions, can your teenager recover? If not, then you need to establish boundaries.

You can also judge by the financial costs or risks, whether they are your responsibilities or your teenagers'. If the financial risks are too great, then you should establish boundaries. You can also judge the seriousness by the spiritual impact. Spirituality is a personal decision, but you can still establish boundaries when you think that your teens' spirituality is threatened or compromised. Such boundaries enhance the growth and development of their spiritual lives.

Finally, boundaries should be appropriate for various stages of life. Some call these stages "markers." By definition, markers are those events in teens' lives that indicate signs that they are maturing or growing up. Markers involve social acknowledgement, along with new responsibilities, new freedoms, and new restraints. Such markers may be getting a driver's license, graduating from high school, or turning eighteen. Young people look forward to markers; once achieved, they give teens the satisfaction that they are progressing towards maturity. Even Jesus himself experienced markers in his life: "And Jesus grew in wisdom and stature, and in favor with God and men" (Luke 2:52). Four distinct areas are indicated in this one verse: Jesus grew intellectually, physically, socially, and spiritually. Established boundaries will vary simply because teenagers are in various stages of their lives. Boundaries will lessen the stress that teenagers face and keep them from making inappropriate decisions.

I have had students in my youth groups and in my classes who have been on the other extreme. They had no boundaries. Yet the very thing they desired in their life was some kind of boundary lines. I was surprised to learn that one of my college students was raised by a lesbian mother and her partner. Yet, this young man is one of my better, more intellectual students. He is also a black belt in karate and is engaged to another one of my students. In spite of the lack of moral boundaries in his home, he has decided to live with his own God-inspired boundaries.

The university where I teach has rules that students agree to live by while attending the school. Both the boundaries and the consequences are clear. Some students find them easy to live by, while others find them difficult. Typically, the students who have difficulty come from less regulated or nonregulated households.

I've had a hobby over the years that I enjoy—basketball officiating. I like to get into the heat of the game right on the court, rather than watch it from the stands. Whether it is an NCAA or NBA basketball game, I always watch the referees. When the players get on the court, they can have a great time playing basketball. But a black line around the perimeter of the court is called a boundary line. Players can have a great game within the boundaries, but once their feet step on or over the line, they must give up the ball, the consequence of crossing the boundary.

When you establish boundaries for your teenagers, they can have a great and safe time within those boundaries. Unfortunately, they often step over those lines inadvertently or on purpose. Regardless, there should be consequences.

Corporal punishment? No, not for teenagers.

Restrictions and groundings? Yes.

Like what? Taking away cell phones, computers, money, car keys, or social events but not from church or youth events.

Be careful how you react when your teen crosses boundaries. If you become angry, then your teen will not come to you in a more serious crisis.

I once made a deal with my daughter that if she ever felt uncomfortable in a situation or with an individual, she could call me at any time. I would pick her up with no questions asked. Of course, she could tell me anything she wanted to, and we could sensibly talk about it. She took me up on it once, and things worked out. When your teenagers do find themselves in a situation, don't you want to be the person they run to?

Boundaries have never been a popular topic with teenagers. At an age where appropriate freedom for your teenagers can be a balancing act, you are precariously perched between giving too much freedom too early (which can be dangerous), while withholding appropriate freedom (which can be debilitating). Yet without a doubt, teenagers tend to flourish when they know the boundaries. They understand all the benefits of staying within those boundaries and the consequences of straying outside of them.

chapter 6

Modeling

Modeling is something that I've always wrestled with, not the concept but the peripheral assumptions that I have to be perfect all the time. Vulnerability is something that goes along with modeling. Although I strive to be a good model for my kids, I am still in process.

Our teens are not looking for perfection. Instead they want models who strive to get it right, who admit mistakes, and who make appropriate corrections.

What Modeling Looks Like

Your mere presence at your teens' events is a great start in modeling. Reschedule your meetings and tell those involved why. Most people will understand and rearrange their schedules with you. Attend your teens' sporting events, recitals, plays, and performances, whether they are first string, first chair, sitting on the bench, or whatever. And when you're there, be there. Leave your laptop in the trunk. Cell phones are okay, but keep your eyes on your teens. Make sure they see you! Get in their line of sight, for they will be looking for your nods of approval.

While politicians have talking points, parents have bragging points. Events that your teens are involved in make great bragging points. You may brag at the office or at church, but bragging around the meal table is especially gratifying for your teenagers. It does wonders for their struggling self-esteem as well as their relationships with you. Your presence tells them that they are more important than your job or your responsibilities. Of course, you should tell them that you must work to provide for their needs. Obviously, you can't be there for every event on their calendars and when you can't, let them know why. They'll understand. Just don't make missing a habit.

Modeling also involves assisting your teenagers in the pursuit of their dreams or goals no matter how insignificant. You can help by verbal encouragement, your research of their dreams/goals to provide informed decisions with regards to their further involvement, financial support of camps, courses, clinics, and finally, getting them there. If it is over the edge for you, then talk about it. Steer them into something more appropriate but still interesting to them. The benefits include achieving some of those dreams/goals. Talk about a good feeling, a sense of fulfillment, and the joy of accomplishment. With those victories, you are setting your teenagers up knowing what achievement feels like. Even more important is what it takes to get there. They will see the benefits of hard work and effort.

The Scriptures have a little word with a big meaning: *add* (2 Pet. 1:5). Oswald Chambers says:

> "Add" means there is something we have to do. We are in danger of forgetting that we cannot do what God does, and that God will not do what we can do. We cannot save ourselves nor sanctify ourselves, God does that; but God

> will not give us good habits, He will not give us character, He will not make us walk aright. We have to do all that ourselves, we have to work out the salvation God has worked in. "Add" means to get into the habit of doing things, and in the initial stages it is difficult. To take the initiative is to make a beginning, to instruct yourself in the way you have to go.[1]

Teenagers need to learn the important exercises of planning ahead, prioritizing, saving, and even strategic thinking, exercises that will go a long way in preparing them for their adult futures. My wife and I have seen some dreams or goals come and go with our teenagers. Their goals have usually been in the form of sports—basketball, snowboarding, volleyball, and other sports. We have spent hours in the gym, waiting in the car when the team arrives late, spending money, rearranging schedules, and driving them here and there. Then their dreams shifted to educational goals. The ages of my vehicles prove that we spent our money on education.

While we've been focusing on extrinsic dreams or goals, we, as parents, also need to focus more on intrinsic goals. Jerry Jenkins in his book, *Twelve Things I Want My Kids to Remember,* put it this way:

> The avenues to success may all sound good. Take care of your body. Get plenty of sleep. Eat right. Get up early. Read a lot. Write a lot. Know how to talk to people. Learn to sell yourself and your product. Learn to deal with difficult people. Overcome objections. Break down resistance. Work harder. Work smarter. Build a network. Learn to negotiate. Trade favors. Dress right, look right, talk right.
>
> You do all the above because it will bring you what you've always wanted. Notice. Wealth. Success. Self-satisfaction. Leisure time. The ability to travel, to have no financial worries, to be somebody!

> Hear me, boys, I would be proud to see you achieve all that, as long as those were not your goals. Those goals would disappoint me. No, those goals would break my heart. Those goals would tell me where your heart is, and it wouldn't be where God wants it to be.
>
> There is nothing, nothing, nothing wrong with a person's being an achiever or even what society interestingly and probably incorrectly calls an overachiever. God may call you to be famous, a leader, or a wealthy, influential person of independent means. What a responsibility! What an ominous duty! And if you get there because of pure motives and goals, I'll be behind you 100 percent.
>
> I say this before God, however: if you raise a family on a lower middle-class income because you're a servant of Christ, if you never own a second car, if you can't dress in the latest fashions or take your family out to dinner, let alone entertain anyone else, I will be every bit as proud of you.
>
> Your goals should be intrinsic. Make it your goal to be the best you can be at whatever task is set before you.
>
> I want to be the best I can be at whatever I am doing, not so that will make me the best in the world and bring me all the goodies outlined above. Rather, I want to present to God a fully exercised measure of that which He has entrusted to me.[2]

Are your own goals intrinsic? The Bible says to "offer your bodies as living sacrifices, holy and pleasing to God" (Rom. 12:1). The parable in Matthew 25:14–30 reminds us that whatever God gives us, we are responsible to develop and invest it. The return is that God entrusts us with more. How have you done? It's never too late to start (again). Remember, your kids are watching.

Modeling involves loosening your grip on your teenagers. This may go completely contrary to what you would like to do. The harsh reality is that many parents whose "tweenagers" are becoming teenagers, begin to panic. Perhaps both parents and kids were slack during the preteen years, without too many challenges or questions. In other words, parents had a loose grip on their preteens and now tighten their grip. Others panic because they had a tight grip on their preteens, and since that seemed to work, they tighten the grip even more. Both approaches are wrong.

This is not the time to tighten the grip. Obviously, the opposite extreme is to have no grip, which is equally wrong. But adolescence is the time to loosen up on your grip. This is not a reason to relinquish your parental duties and responsibilities, but it is a wake-up call to be fully engaged in the lives of your teenagers, whether with school, sports, friends, boyfriends, girlfriends, work, or church. This engagement is a balance between giving appropriate freedoms in some areas and withholding them in others. Premature freedoms can be dangerous, while appropriate freedoms withheld can be debilitating. Now you and your teens can discuss issues with civility, experience, and common sense. As parents of teenagers, you now move from all-knowing parents to consultants or advisors. For instance, curfew can be a sensitive matter. Find an acceptable common ground, within reason, that the teens and you can live with. Remember, be engaged, but don't remove your hands completely. You can take your hands off about a lot of things, but in the meantime, foster relationships that will keep you knowledgeable about your teens.

Relinquishing some of your responsibilities and passing them on to your teenagers is a big step in being the right model for them. This is not something to be taken lightly but still needs to be done. Parents who have embraced their parental responsibilities with enthusiasm should embrace relinquishment with equal enthusiasm. Give teens those household chores that you have held on to dearly. They may not do them the way you do it, so bite your tongue, and applaud their efforts—not necessarily their efficiency or effectiveness. Once you've gotten past their effort, then work on the way jobs were done. You need to applaud their effort, while their mistakes become learning experiences. With this approach their next effort will be much improved and will soon meet your standards. An even bigger issue for teenagers is the fact that you are imparting higher levels of respect and trust. Respect and trust go a long way in the transition from teen to adult years.

On the flip side, teenagers will get a lesson in losing your respect when they knowingly disregard your wishes. At the same time they will learn how hard it is to reinstate that trust. Should there be consequences for deliberately doing something wrong? Definitely. But they must be objective consequences, not emotional outbursts. If the situations become too emotionally charged, your teenagers will be reluctant to try again. This can be crippling. If you get it wrong, do what Ross Campbell says in his book, *Relational Parenting*:

> Finally, model forgiveness. You teach by example how to forgive and how to find forgiveness from God and other people. You do this first by forgiving and by asking for forgiveness—of your spouse or even your child—when you make a mistake.
>
> Yes, if you wrong your child, you should ask for your child's forgiveness. I cannot overemphasize how important this is. At the point when you are angry and don't feel like asking for forgiveness from your child, try to remember this truth: True intimacy comes from resolved conflict. You can even come to regard conflict as an opportunity to draw closer to one another—if you manage your anger and can lead family members to a loving resolution of the problem.[3]

So get a grip on your emotions. Be an adult. The more responsibility you give your teen, the more they will be prepared for adulthood.

Finally, be a good model of parenting by listening, really listen. Adults have a difficult time listening. Maybe they're too busy or preoccupied. Or maybe they have more "important" things to deal with. But listening is a skill you can learn. If teens get the impression that you are not listening to them, they will not waste their time talking to you. Yet, this is one of parents' biggest gripes: that their teenagers don't talk. So when they do talk, listen. Take advantage of this communication opportunity. One in three teens in this country says he or she rarely has a conversation with a parent that lasts longer than fifteen minutes.[4]

To get better at listening, check yourself. What does your posture say? Does it say that you are interested in what your teens are saying or that you are not the least bit interested? Stop what you are doing, if you can. If you can't, ask them to wait a moment until you can listen. Now lean forward; turn away from the computer; turn off the television. Look at your teens. Stay focused on them, their projects, or their papers. Concentrate. Once they've finished talking, and you need clarification, repeat what you think you heard. If you didn't get it right, they'll let you know. Select the best time to listen for you and for them but mostly for them. If it's late at night, stay up. If it's at a restaurant, then go out with them more often. Listening is basic to communication and relationships. So if you're not good at it, work to get better.

No one is saying to strive for perfection. Many times you get better by trial and error. But it is a big step when you admit that you need help. I haven't been to an Alcoholics Anonymous meeting, but I know attendees must introduce themselves by saying, "My name is so-and-so, and I'm an alcoholic." So admit that you need help at parenting. Don't be afraid to say so, whether it's to each other, other parents, your own parents, a pastor, a youth pastor, or a counselor. The first step towards getting any help is admitting you need it. Remember, you are among friends.

chapter 7

Issues[1]

God says, "For it is shameful even to mention what the disobedient do in secret" (Eph. 5:12). Frankly, this is why we have struggled with describing current issues facing teens. Unfortunately, when living and working with teenagers, we need to be familiar with what tempts them, what they're involved in, or who is preying upon them. Instead of being naive, we need to speak knowledgeably.

The following are descriptions of trends or disturbing behaviors that were not included in our first book. Some have had their share of press, while others are recently raising their ugly heads. Hopefully, these descriptions will give you enough information to help you converse with young people from a position of knowledge and understanding. For a more extensive list of disturbing behaviors, see our book, *Disturbing Behavior: 53 Alarming Trends of Teens and How to Spot Them* (AMG Publishers).

1. Teen Magazines

In her book *Wear Sunscreen: A Primer for Real Life*, May Schmich says,

> Enjoy the power and beauty of your youth. Oh, never mind. You will not understand the power and beauty of your youth until they've faded. But trust me, in 20 years you'll look back at photos of yourself and recall in a way you can't grasp now how much possibility lay before you and how fabulous you really looked. You are not as fat as you imagine . . . Do not read beauty magazines. They will only make you feel ugly.[2]

"I'm in Love with My Best Friend."
"100 Supercute Swimsuits."
"The Hottest Guys of the Summer."
"Jesse McCartney—What Turns Him On?"
"I Gave Up My Baby."

These are the titles of cover-feature articles for an issue of one of today's most popular teen magazines, *Teen People.* The brightly colored cover has these flashy titles, along with others to catch millions of teenage girls' attention. As most know, the teenage years are a period of change and growth. These are the years of "revelation, awakening emotions, and newly discovered capabilities."[3] Teenagers are growing out of childhood into adult life. They need direction and guidance. Where are they turning? Girls especially seek answers from teen magazines, such as *YM*, *Seventeen*, *CosmoGirl*, *Teen*, and *Elle Girl*.

How influential are these magazines? Surely, teenagers can think for themselves as they exercise their analytical and abstract thinking. Not true. Popular teen magazines are not only addictive but also destructive.

Teen magazines make ridiculous attempts to answer teen issues. In a recent contest, teens entered advertisements for teen pregnancy prevention. All the ads claimed that abstinence is the best prevention, but if teens do have sex, they need to use protection. Abstinence is the best prevention; there is no argument there. Then why does this same magazine encourage sex by featuring half-naked male models and girls modeling immodest fashions?

According to *Group Magazine*, about 50 percent of teenagers have had sex by the time they turn eighteen years old.[4] Teen magazines confuse young adults who try to determine their self-worth and ask themselves how far is too far.

> If the screaming pink and orange cover lines on mass-circulation teen magazines don't get to you, the mixed messages inside will. Has there ever before been a flood of such contradictory, confusing high-pressure "advice" directed at teen girls that serves their interests less?
>
> The ying and yang of being simultaneously irresistible and virginal fill page after page. Impressionable teens (and preteens) are being whip-sawed by the mixed messages. Tips on how to look hot and sneak lip-locks with a beau at the school locker are interspersed with warnings to keep sexual matters from getting out of hand.[5]

As teenagers come out of childhood, their relationships with their parents change. Most teens no longer feel comfortable to ask their parents for answers. One place they can go to ask questions is a magazine. Most teen magazines offer a question-answer section. In an issue of *Teen People*, teens asked questions about privacy from their parents, siblings, and friends.[6] Although these articles may not always be wrong, they are not always right. Your adolescents need to find these answers in God's Word, for "All Scripture is God-breathed and is useful for teaching, rebuking, correcting and training in righteousness, so that the man of God may be thoroughly equipped for every good work" (2 Tim. 3:16).

In addition to articles, surveys, and quizzes, teen magazines usually have horoscope pages. I am not sure how many young people buy into these horoscopes, but some teens read them and believe that these predictions cause circumstances in their lives. They are reading and believing lies. All teenagers should be given the opportunity to hear that God loves them. "'For I know the plans I have for you,' declares the Lord, 'plans to prosper you and not to harm you, plans to give you hope and a future'" (Jer. 29:11).

Yet another misconception of today's teen pop magazines is the portrayal of celebrities so called *perfect* and glamorous lifestyles. Although most celebrities seem to have it made, the media, including these magazines, leave out the broken and confused lives that many stars have today. An article entitled "Celeb Gossip" describes Paris Hilton's success as a model, actress, singer, and fashion designer.[7] This deception of the perfect and successful life causes teens to look to these stars as role models. Trust me, you do not want most celebrities to have such influence on your adolescents. Teens' views on life will become distorted. If they follow celebrity lifestyles, they may fall into the same sins as their role models. You need to teach your young people to "fix [their] eyes on Jesus, the author and perfector of our faith" (Heb. 12:2), rather than on people who will lead them down the road of destruction and death.

Adolescence is supposed to be a time of extreme growth in all areas, including knowledge. Teens begin to think abstractly and ask questions before accepting ideas, but teen magazines question their intelligence. Do they need quizzes to figure out "which spring trend was made for you," or "Do you need to repair your rep.?"[8] By taking these simple multiple-choice quizzes, teenage girls can find out:

- if their crushes are true love,
- if they are too shy,
- what kind of kissers they are,
- about their stress levels, and
- what type of boys they like.

First of all, these matters do not increase their knowledge. Second, can they really narrow issues into three options? And lastly, do the conclusions even help teenage girls?

2. Huffing

Ricky was on summer break from high school when his father came home and found him lying dead on his bedroom floor. Ricky had been "huffing," or inhaling household chemicals to attain a dizzy high. What had started out as seemingly harmless fun suddenly turned deadly. Ricky and his friend had been "taking turns pulling a Freon-filled bag off each other's head. When Ricky died, he was alone; no one was there to pull the bag off. He died instantly of cardiac arrest in what's often referred to as sudden sniffing death syndrome."[9]

Unfortunately, Ricky's story is not isolated. Many adolescents have tried or soon will try inhalant abuse before they reach adulthood. While drug use seems to be on the decline among teens, inhalant abuse is on the rise. Inhalants are the fourth most abused substances in the United States among eighth, tenth, and twelfth graders. Alcohol, tobacco, and marijuana are the top three, according to the Monitoring the Future Study of 2000. There are many reasons for this. Over one thousand products can be used to get a high and most of these are readily accessible and legal. Not much attention has been given to this problem. While educators talk about drugs and alcohol usage, many do not address the issue of inhalant abuse. Teens see it as harmless because the inhalants used in huffing are common. Inhalants are also cheaper and easier to obtain than "real" drugs. While illegal drugs are often hard to come by in rural areas, inhalants exist in abundance.

"Inhalant abuse, commonly called huffing, is the purposeful inhalation of chemical vapors to achieve an altered mental or physical state, which for most abusers is a euphoric effect."[10] While many inhalant abusers are adolescents, some adults also abuse inhalants. The reasons for usage vary somewhat between these two groups. While most adolescents use inhalants to get a euphoric high, many adults use them to enhance their sexual experience.

Adolescents mainly use volatile solvents, aerosols, and gases. Volatile solvents are liquids that vaporize at room temperature if left in unsealed containers. These include paint thinners, gasoline, correction fluid, felt-tip markers, nail polish and remover, and glue. Aerosols are sprays such as paint, deodorant, hair products, cooking products, and fabric protectors. Silver and gold spray paint are particularly popular among inhalant abusers. Gases are substances that have no definite shape or volume. They include gases found in butane lighters, air-conditioning units, and propane tanks, as well as medical anesthetics, such as ether, chloroform, and nitrous oxide. It is easy to see why teens use and abuse these products rather than illegal drugs. They're cheap and easily accessible.

As mentioned above, many adults use inhalants to enhance their sexual experiences. To do this they use nitrates, which include three basic types: "Cyclohexyl nitrite is found in room deodorizers. Amyl nitrite comes in small, mesh-covered, sealed capsules that are popped or snapped in order to release the vapors. Because of this popping or snapping, these capsules are frequently called poppers or snappers. Butyl nitrite is often sold in small bottles that, like amyl nitrite capsules, are referred to as poppers. Nitrites are available in adult bookstores and shops and over the Internet."[11]

Inhalant abuse goes by many names among teens and adults. Some of the more common names are *amys*, *bang*, *bolt*, *boppers*, *bullet*, *climax*, *glading*, *gluey*, *hardware*, *head cleaner*, *hippie crack*, *kick*, *poor man's pot*, and *poppers*.

Whatever name inhalant abuse goes by, it is clear that it is dangerous. Some of the effects on the body include the following:

1. *Brain damage:* Inhalants dissolve the myelin sheath that surrounds the brain cells, resulting in cell death.
2. *Cerebral cortex:* Cellular death causes memory loss, permanent personality changes, and learning disabilities.
3. *Cerebellum:* This controls balance and coordination. Damage causes a loss of coordination and slurred speech. Chronic huffers have tremors and shake violently.
4. *Heart:* Sudden sniffing death syndrome (SSD) may occur because inhalants make the heart beat irregularly and can cause cardiac arrest.

The kidneys, liver, bone marrow, and other organs are also affected. Results similar to fetal alcohol syndrome may also occur when inhalants are used during pregnancy. "It's like Russian roulette. They (huffers) might make it the first but not the tenth or twentieth time, or maybe, the first time their heart bursts," says Leonard Ward of the Pennsylvania Attorney General's office on Drug Demand Reduction.[12] A brain-imaging study, conducted by Brookhaven National

Laboratory, offers clues as to why inhalant use and why solvents, specifically, may be so addictive.[13]

Parents and youth pastors can help combat this problem by educating both themselves and teens on the dangers of inhalant abuse. Keep in mind that this problem can affect anyone; we can't afford to have an "it's not my kid" attitude toward inhalant abuse. The truth is that we can do very little to prevent adolescents from experimenting with inhalants because teens can obtain them easily. Knowledge is power, and if we give them the facts in a straightforward manner, they will be equipped to make good decisions.

Parents and youth pastors also can remind teens that their bodies are the temples of the Holy Spirit and should not be abused. Ephesians 5:18 tells us, "Do not get drunk on wine which leads to debauchery. Instead, be filled with the Spirit." When we become intoxicated, either with alcohol, inhalants, or other substances, we are not being controlled by the Spirit. Since inhalants affect the mind, abusers will often act in ways that are contrary to how they normally act. This is not how believers are to behave. We are to be led by the Spirit and not allow anything else to control us.

3. Teens Abusing Parents

A definition given by the Internet source *www.teamcares.org* states, "The definition of parent abuse is any act of a child that is intended to cause physical, psychological, or financial damage to gain power and control over a parent."[14] In the physical sense, teenagers may hit, punch, or shove. Psychologically, teens will try to make parents feel as if they are crazy. Teenagers will also play mind games with parents. Teenagers may steal their parents' money or sell items belonging to their parents. Teenagers may even try to make their parents buy something they cannot afford.

One fifteen-year-old boy used his mother as a "punching bag" every time he did not get his way. His teachers had no problem with the boy and found him to be a good student. But his view was, "If Daddy can beat Mummy why can't I?"[15] The mother's sister asked people for advice on what she could recommend to calm this boy down. Apparently, the husband beat his wife and blamed her for not being able to handle the teen.

Although this disturbing behavior is not as common as other behaviors among teenagers, statistics back up the stories. Researchers have found that children physically abuse an estimated 2.5 million parents every year, according to the *Halifax Herald*. This newspaper also stated, "Often, mom is the victim. Girls as young as ten may emerge as early abusers, though older teenage abusers are usually boys, who exploit their physical size."[16] Of the 2.5 million parents abused every year, 900,000 are severely beaten. A family with this problem approached nine different counselors for help. Often a mother will go back, second guess herself, and think that it is her fault.

To cope with this problem, parents should speak out about what is going on in their households. Support groups where parents can talk out their difficulties are helpful. Mediators between the teenagers and the parents work well. Some say it's necessary to discipline children at a young age to let them know that this behavior is not tolerated. "I do not agree on any kind of physical punishment, not at all! But this has also caused a problem amongst parents on how to punish their child in a way that 'society' will accept as proper."[17] Proverbs 22:6 says, "Train a child in the way he should go, and when he is old he will not turn from it."

4. Drug Dealers in School

In the past, teens could only find drugs in forbidden neighborhoods through "local" dealers. Today, however, 51 percent of high schoolers who use drugs buy them from friends after class.[18] Student dealers have become one of the leading dangers facing schools today.

The first question is: where do kids get the drugs? Students may seek suppliers to lend or "front" them supplies of drugs. In this form of dealing, suppliers give a certain amount of drugs to the sellers and expect a certain amount of money to be given back at a given date. With the lack of money being a problem in the first place, the lending of drugs is the most prevalent way students will start. Another less common way for students to start dealing is to use their own money. With over 1.5 million citizens being arrested every year for either possessing or selling drugs, it takes little effort for interested students to find a source.[19]

To fully understand this issue, parents and counselors must understand why students become involved in such activities. Beyond the cultural and psychological issues that draw many into this behavior, drug dealing seems attractive to many teens. They live in a materialistic world that screams that the newest shoes, clothing, and electronics are musts in order to fit in with their peers. The problem is that these items may cost hundreds of dollars, and most parents cannot afford them. Therefore, teens will do whatever it takes to obtain the necessary money to fulfill their desires.

Oddly enough, for many kids, money is simply an added benefit aside from the main reason they indulge in this behavior. When children enter into their teen years, they are overwhelmed by the need to belong and be part of something. This is why the mafia-like lifestyle of the drug-dealing world seems so appealing. Suppliers bring students into their homes, offering money, protection, prestige, and social environments for anyone to envy. It is normal for a supplier to have ten or so users all in the same house for hours playing video games, using drugs, or listening to music.

Young people tend to look only at the positive outcomes of their decisions and overlook the bad consequences. Sadly enough, in spite of the glamour, popularity, and comfort, most dealers suffer some consequences. Some of the worse repercussions are mental. First, dealers become accustomed to having money. Once they quit, they have to work legitimately for the first time. Often they find this too difficult, and will fall back into selling again. If their only point in life is to make money, why stop? Also, dealers are in lifestyles that cause them to hate authority. They resent police and other authoritative figures even years after they stop dealing.

On a less severe level, dealers have to regain trusting relationships with parents, friends, and their communities. However, dealers some times experience emotional scars that go deeper. Murder, robbery, and violence go hand in hand with dealing.[20] Student dealers may be involved in such situations, which they will have to carry with them forever. Look in any town's newspapers, and you will undoubtedly find violent acts traced back to drugs.[21]

Although the emotional consequences seem devastating, the physical consequences are even harsher. Since violent acts are common in drug dealing, student dealers may be harmed or even murdered.[22] The consequences become permanent. Families also suffer a great deal of pain and loss, a price that money cannot repay.

While murder is common in the society of dealers, the side effects from drug use is the number one downside to this lifestyle. Student dealers have endless access and peer pressure to use drugs. They do not understand how drugs will affect them even decades after discontinued use. Permanent brain damage, lung cancer, heart trouble, mental delusions, and kidney damage are just a few of the side effects they may experience.[23]

In a national survey done by the National Institute of Drug Abuse, 60 percent of students said that drugs are used or sold in their schools.[24] So parents, youth leaders, and teachers must be informed and capable of identifying the problem. They should observe any changes in their teens, especially socially. They must be cautious if their kids befriend older teens or adults and are hesitant to introduce them. Parents and youth workers must also know the current phrases that are commonly used. *X*, *green*, *snow*, *blues*, *triple stacks*, or *kitty* are terms used to describe any drug from marijuana, ecstasy, or cocaine. *Adam* is no longer Eve's husband, and *triple stacks* are not pancakes.[25] Parents need to listen their teens' conversations and be aware of these terms. They should especially be on the lookout if their kids show up with new clothes and other possessions that they could not normally afford. Simply put: parents need to be involved.

On the spiritual front, youth groups must be on guard when it comes to current or former dealers. Dealers lacked acceptance or families, which got them started in drugs in the first place. They need to realize Christ's church is there for them. Since many struggle with money issues, youth pastors must be ready with Christ's answers as means to guide. Dealers need to realize God will take care of them, and no matter what happens everything will be all right. Jesus said, "Therefore I tell you, do not worry about your life, what you will eat or drink; or about your body, what you will wear" (Matt. 6:25).

Youth leaders need to know where to send dealers if they are addicted to drugs and need treatment to recover. On the other hand, dealers may still be involved in drug dealing, and youth leaders need to know how to handle such situations. Be the shepherd of your young flock thinking of the safety and well-being of the whole group, but you may want to give dealers a chance to quit and start new lives. However, police may need to become involved for one of two reasons:

- dealers refuse to quit, and it is the youth leaders' lawful responsibility to turn them in, or
- dealers feel they cannot quit because of threatening relationships with the suppliers. This is unusual, but parents and youth leaders should be ready to face anything.

5. Identity Theft by Teenagers

Computer crime is a new issue that no other generation has had to deal with. However, we all will have to accept it and learn how to protect ourselves from it. This crime is quick, easy, and can be done at home in front of a computer. One major component of computer crime is identity theft.[26] The FBI refers to this crime as "the fastest growing white-collar crime in America."[27] Nothing sounds better to teenagers than having limitless amounts of money and not having to pay a single cent back. Because of this new appeal, identity theft is on the rise among teens.

Recently, seventeen-year-old Troy Vaughn Davis of Rocky Mount, North Carolina, was charged with one hundred fifteen counts of "financial identity fraud and obtaining property by false pretense." Davis is accused of attempting to steal merchandise worth over one hundred thousand dollars. More specifically, he is being prosecuted for stealing the identities of dozens of local citizens and then applying for and receiving credit cards that were issued in the names of those victims. Furthermore, Davis is also "accused of stealing mail from residential boxes and using the information to assume the victims' identities." Police finally caught onto Davis' scam in November of 2004.[28]

Being a victim of identity theft is easier than most people think. All that a thief needs is "your driver's license, checking account or credit card number, Social Security number or even just your wireless phone."[29] Some simple tips to protect yourself from identity theft are to keep your birth certificate and Social Security card in a safe place, not on you. Do not loan your cell phone, driver's license, checkbook, or credit cards to anyone. These should be kept in a safe place. Shred all documents with personal information such as bank-account numbers, your home address, and your mother's maiden name. Unless you are positive that you are dealing with a reputable organization, do not give personal information over the phone or the Internet. Before applying for student loans or your first apartment, check your credit report thoroughly. Also, when going to college, make sure that your Social Security number does not double as your student identification number. By following these simple steps, you can protect yourself from identity theft. It is easier to prevent identity theft than to try to prove your innocence later.[30]

The National Cyber Security Alliance (NCSA) in 2004 reported that of Americans under the age of twenty-five, 40 percent believed that it would be more probable for them to be struck by lightning, to be audited by the IRS, or to win the lottery than to be victims of computer-security problems.[31] According to the U.S. National Weather Service, the odds of being hit by lightning are 0.0000102 percent. In reality, approximately 70 percent of computer users are in some way affected by "cybersecurity threats, including viruses, phishing scams, and hacking."[32] The Federal Trade Commission reported that almost ten million people were victimized by identity theft in 2004.[33]

Phishing scams are also on the rise. In October, November, and December, 2004, the numbers of active phishing sites reported were 1,142, 1,518, and 1,707 respectively. Many phishing Websites use Trojan horses (software programs that hide in files attached to e-mails or are downloaded from the Internet and installed on one's computer) to gain most of their information. When used in identity theft, most of these programs are used in the form of a keystroke-logger (a key-logger is a program that runs in the background, recording all keystrokes). Once keystrokes are logged, they are hidden in the machine for later retrieval or shipped raw to the attacker. After a computer is infected with the keystroke-logger program, the attacker will search for useful information such as passwords or other personal information.[34]

In the summer of 2003, a Pennsylvania teenager used a keystroke-logging program to capture "the typing activity of any user that downloaded it and periodically e-mailed it back to the teen." The teen "contacted several members of a financial Website, alerting them to the availability of a new stock-charting tool." Through the keystroke-logging program, the teen gained access to the online brokerage account of an investor. Then, the teen discovered the investor's brokerage account number and password. With this information, the teen "proceeded to execute a series of options trades that wiped out almost all the investor's cash holdings." Criminal and civil actions have been taken against this individual.[35]

Another teen, eighteen-year-old Shiva Sharma of Queens, New York, was charged with stealing the identities of over one hundred America Online customers. He allegedly got credit cards in the victims' names and charged over ten thousand dollars worth of merchandise, consisting of electronic equipment and racing-car parts. He created a phony Website that appeared to be an AOL site. According to the authorities, he then "e-mailed the customers, telling them their billing information had been lost and asking them to reply with their personal data." This fraudulent site resulted in over one hundred responses from AOL customers. He took the stolen information and got credit and debit cards in the customers' names with a value of five hundred thousand dollars. Even though pleading innocent, he was found guilty. Sharma faced a twelve-count indictment. His charges "included charges of identity theft, grand larceny, and falsifying business records." Sharma could face up to seven years in prison. He was the first person to be charged under New York's new identity theft law that took effect in November 2002.[36] This new law considers identity theft a felony.[37]

Therefore, identity theft is a growing concern. Many tech-savvy teens are being drawn into illegal acts for easy money. We must not only protect ourselves from such crimes, but we must also inform young people of the severity and harsh consequences of these actions. Identity theft is not a laughing matter.

6. Mimicking Stunts Seen on Television

Today's generation is one that thrives on excitement. Teens will seemingly engage in any behavior for the sheer thrill value. Sadly, many seek to quench this adrenaline thirst by performing dangerous stunts. Kids all over the nation have made their new hobby mimicking stunts they see on TV and consequently becoming seriously hurt. The media and society as a whole have passively accepted this behavior. Most notorious are the ESPN's *X-Games*, *Extreme Championship Wrestling* (ECW), MTV's *Jackass*, and now *FCF* (full-contact fighting).

First, we will focus on the media event that has the highest number of injuries following it: the *X-Games*. In the early 1990s, ESPN launched *X-Games* for the first time. These broadcasts were ESPN's answer to the nation's growing need to view extreme sports. These sports included skateboarding, Rollerblading, bicycle riding, snowboarding, surfing, snow skiing, dirt-bike racing, all-terrain-vehicle (ATV) racing, and jet-ski racing. The stunts kids see in these telecasts include flipping dirt bikes, jumping twenty feet in the air with skateboards, jumping off cliffs on snowboards, and riding down one-hundred foot rails on Rollerblades. Teens see these stunts and try to copy them, but they need to realize that the athletes are professionally trained and that the terrain they perform on is professionally built, prepared, and groomed. Viewers will find playgrounds, parks, ski slopes, mountains, handrails, or other various buildings for their bases.

Soon after the extreme-sports craze hit our nation, the wrestling world followed suit with the emergence of *Extreme Championship Wrestling* or *ECW*. This form of wrestling took the traditional World Wrestling Entertainment (WWE) and added stunts that were more dangerous in nature. These stunts included shooting flares at others, lighting people on fire, jumping on top of people from heights up to twenty-five feet, breaking chairs and bats over people's heads, or the most popular stunt: body slamming someone on top of ten or more tables stacked on top of each other. What many of the viewers do not realize is that these stunts are professionally staged. The wrestlers have been through stunt academies, and the props are specifically designed for the stunts. Viewers forget that professional wrestling is not real and try to mimic the behavior on each other. Trampolines, mats, or bed mattresses are used as bases for kids to try their own rendition of *ECW*, nicknamed "backyard wrestling." Kids will jump off their houses onto each other, break wooden objects over each others' heads, and toss each other off various tall structures. This behavior has decreased in popularity over the past few years but is still practiced enough to cause concern.

Although extreme sports cause the highest number of injuries, MTV's *Jackass* has been by far the worst influence on kids who try to copy TV's destructive behavior. This show first premiered in 2000 where the main premise was to embark on whatever daredevil stunt came to the actors' minds. This show became intriguing because the stunts were real, as was the pain. Stars performed stunts, such as riding wheelchairs down mountains, lighting each other on fire, hitting each other in the privates, blowing firecrackers up in each others' noses and mouths, or flipping go-carts. This show became so popular that in 2003 MTV launched *Jackass: The Movie*. Sadly enough, this show grossed over sixty-four million dollars in ticket sales in just the U.S. alone. The show was banned early in 2004, but since then the actors have split off to release many new videos of the same nature.

When it comes to figuring out the consequences of these behaviors, they are as obvious as the blood-covered shirts and doctors' bills that follow. Physical injury is hands down the worst resulting factor. The stunts kids perform are so extreme in nature, hospitalization occurs almost every time something goes wrong.[38] Usually, these injuries simply involve stitches or casts, but many times the injuries are permanent, and the teens never recover fully.[39] Thus, five minutes of excitement has ruined the rest of their lives.

So what can parents and youth ministers do to steer teens away from these types of behaviors? Telling them that their bodies are the temples of God may be true, but what teenage boys do not feel that they are invincible? The problem is that watching *X-Games* or *ECW* is not inherently wrong, nor is under the right circumstances, performing these stunts wrong. It is first necessary to educate the youth about the reality of these sports. They need to realize a lot happens behind the scenes that the viewers do not see.

However, even with educating them, teens still need extreme excitement in their lives. Youth ministers and parents have to offer avenues for young people to get their adrenaline fixes. Paintball, white-water rafting, and rock climbing are just a few ways parents or youth workers can show teens that they can have an awesome time in other ways. Leaders today need to realize that this behavior is not going away, and the generations coming up will need even higher levels of excitement in their lives.

7. Anger

Teenagers tend to be emotional, and anger is one emotion they will display. Anger becomes an issue because of the way teens choose to handle it. With a few exceptions, adults tend to think logically through problems and make appropriate decisions on how to deal with their anger. Teenagers, on the other hand, do not think through problems as thoroughly and often make unwise decisions. Adults often express their anger by yelling, which is far healthier for them as well as the people around them. But teenagers often make rash decisions in their anger that hurt themselves or those around them. Although it's not wrong to be angry, it's wrong and sinful to express anger in a violent manner that is harmful to others. Focus Adolescents Services says, "Its [teen anger] expressions can include physical and verbal violence, prejudice, malicious gossip, antisocial behavior, sarcasm, addictions, withdrawals, and psychosomatic disorders." [40] Teens see examples in movies, TV, and even in real life and decide to take revenge. They act out rashly what they think is acceptable.

We often hear stories about students who go to school with guns and shoot classmates and teachers. These teens target students who made fun of them for being different or for no reason at all. Other times shooters are so angry that they shoot at random and ruin other people's lives.

Thirteen-year-old Nathaniel Brazill was sent home from school for throwing water balloons. This discipline enraged him. He wanted to talk to a couple girls, one who it's said, he had a crush on. The teacher, Barry Grunow, however, would not allow him to speak with the girls, so Nathaniel pulled a gun on Grunow, and killed him. As part of his sentence, Nathaniel was required to take anger-management classes. He faces up to twenty-eight years in prison.

The bloodiest school shooting since the Columbine shooting in 1999 occurred at Red Lake High School in Minnesota. This was the second fatal shooting to happen in Minnesota within an eighteen-month time frame. Jeff Weise, the shooter at Red Lake High, was said to be obsessed with violence and exhibited antisocial behavior. Apparently, he was not angry with any one person so shot at random. A surviving student told a news reporter that he could hear Jeff talking in the next room asking a boy if he believed in God before he shot and killed him. In other situations at the school, Jeff smiled, waved at fellow students, and then shot them.

Before the incident, Jeff posted comments on Nazi forums and other Websites[41] with stories about characters shooting people with M-16s.[42] Jeff weighed about two hundred and fifty pounds so kids often teased him. He may have felt as if no one in the world cared for him, so he decided to take revenge. To avoid jail time he killed himself after his shooting spree.

Anger can have devastating consequences. According to Focus Adolescence Services, "This [anger] can devastate lives—destroying relationships, harming others, disrupting work, clouding effective thinking, affecting physical health, and ruining futures."[43]

Teenagers develop habits that last a lifetime during this period of growth and development. They may think it is acceptable to express anger in negative forms such as violence, but this can lead to broken homes and even worse. Adults should not think it's normal for teens to act out their anger. If adults learn to recognize the warning signs of out-of-control anger and discipline their teens, many violent events would never happen.

So what does the Bible say about anger? "In your anger do not sin: Do not let the sun go down while you are still angry, and do not give the devil a foothold" (Eph. 4:26–27). The Bible tells us not to sin in our anger, not to hold on to our anger, and not to give the devil a foothold by being angry.

Anger in our hearts produces bitterness; and God doesn't want Christians to hold bitterness toward one another. Scripture tells us, "My dear brothers, take note of this: Everyone should be quick to listen, slow to speak and slow to become angry, for man's anger does not bring about the righteous life that God desires" (James 1:19–20). God wants us to be slow in becoming angry; in other words, we are to be patient with other people. The psalmist says that God is patient with us: "The Lord is compassionate and gracious, slow to anger, abounding in love" (Ps. 103:8). If anyone has the right to be easily angered, it should be God. How many times a day do we fail to live up to his standards? God should be thoroughly irritated with us by now, but is abounding in love.

Christians are called to imitate Christ, meaning we need to love one another and be slow to anger. Jesus showed righteous anger when he saw how God's house had been turned into a den of thieves. In his anger, though, Jesus did not sin. He set an example for us adults, which we need to follow. Then we need to be examples before our teens and expect the same behavior out of them.

8. Sibling Incest

The pristine family portrait hanging in the living room gives the appearance of a happy, functional family unit.

Unfortunately, this façade often belies the ugly truth of abuse. One of the most repulsive examples of this in our culture is sibling incest. It seems inconceivable that in a society as educated as today's soceity that sibling incest would take place. And it's not confined to lower-income or "backwoods" families. People either conceal it or ignore it rather than deal with it properly.

What exactly is sibling incest? "Sibling incest is sexual contact between a sibling dyad (pair) that is experienced by the victim as traumatic."[44] This includes, but is not limited to kissing, fondling, groping, sexual stimulation, exhibition, simulated intercourse, and intercourse between direct siblings or cousins. Due to the disturbing nature of this problem, people are apt to deny that it occurs regularly, but statistics say otherwise. "Incidence of sibling or cousin sexual abuse varies greatly among studies, ranging from 10 percent to 40 percent among those reporting sexual abuse."[45] That sounds unreal, but bear in mind that this is a percentage of those admitting to sexual abuse. "Estimates are that 35 percent of all girls have been sexually abused . . ."[46] So by combining that data, roughly 3 ? percent to 14 percent of all girls have been sexually abused by siblings or cousins. These percentages seem small, but consider that 3 ? percent is roughly one in twenty-five, and that 14 percent is roughly one in seven! The statistics are nearly unbelievable, but the effects of this disturbing behavior are even worse.

Incest is not only devastating to the victims, but it leaves them more vulnerable to other problems. According to Richard Niolon, incest victims are more likely to have a poor self-image, run away, deal with substance abuse, have severe clinical depression, have psychiatric hospitalization, and be at a higher risk for suicide.[47] The troubles for incest victims are endless. They often feel they have no one to talk to about it because they are too ashamed, or they do not want the abusing siblings or cousins to get in trouble. Even if victims tell their parents, often nothing is done to correct the problems. The parents may assume in minor offenses, such as exhibition, kissing, and touching, that there is no real problem and ignore it. In more extreme cases, such as intercourse, the parents may deny it and demand that the victims never speak of it again. So the victims are left to deal with the pain and guilt alone, while the very families that should support them, force them to repress the hurt.

Sometimes incest is merely a symptom of deeper underlying problems. Journalist Ben Goad writes: "A twenty-two-year old Bloomington woman and her seventeen-year-old brother were arrested late Monday on suspicion of felony incest after children playing in an alley found a dead fetus that authorities believe was the pair's stillborn child."[48]

We may assume that these two lived troubled lives, but their example gives some insight as to what kind of environment breeds this behavior. First, the woman had been a ward of the state for most of her childhood with virtually no parental guidance or involvement. Second, even though the seventeen-year-old lived with his parents, the two were often left unsupervised. Lastly, their family thought the woman was a lesbian, so she no doubt felt rejected by those who should be closest to her.

So these three things—no parental involvement, no parental supervision, and no parental acceptance—were all problems that led to this disturbing behavior. How? Look at these in reverse order. If children do not receive love and affection from their parents, they will find it in other places, in this case, from their siblings or cousins. Second, if parents do not properly supervise their children, they create environments for children to explore their natural sexual curiosity in whatever way they choose. And lastly, without parents being involved in their children's lives, behaviors such as this are more likely to happen.

This disturbing behavior underscores the importance of parents in families. Parents must be there for their children emotionally, physically, and spiritually. Their children must feel that they are able to share anything with them. Appropriate touching and embracing from parents can go a long way to preventing this behavior. Good behavior helps teens recognize bad behavior so they can react in proper ways.

9. Autoerotic Asphyxiation

Autoerotic asphyxiation (also known as hypoxyphilia) produces sexual arousal while reducing the oxygen supply to the brain. This is most often a "practice of self-strangulation, typically by the use of a ligature, while masturbating in order to heighten the sexual pleasure as more endorphins are produced when the body reaches the near state of asphyxia.[49]

Autoerotic asphyxiation is usually practiced by individuals alone, not with other individuals. The most common way practitioners obtain hypoxia is through "self-hanging, strangulation, choking, suffocation, and techniques to restrict breathing movements."[50] The most common technique is by self-hanging, which also has the highest number of fatalities.

Partial asphyxia causes practitioners to become unconscious. They then lose control over the means of strangulation, resulting in continued asphyxia and death. Victims often rig some sort of rescue mechanisms that have not worked in the way they anticipated, or they were unable to self-release the devices before they became unconscious. In a few cases, autoerotic asphyxiation has been thought to cause the little-known phenomenon of carotid-sinus reflex death.

The number of deaths in the U. S. from this behavior is misleading due to families and officers misreading suicides that were in actuality deaths from autoerotic asphyxiation.

Most cases are males under forty years of age. However, practicing can begin as young as puberty for some. Most males are found in women's lingerie and are in compromising positions, possibly masturbating. Family members "often hide the evidence of autoerotic death either out of embarrassment or social stigma. These death scene alterations make investigating and classifying of the autoerotic death more difficult."[51]

A former chief FBI agent of serial killers and missing and exploited children explained that police officers often identify situations as suicides rather then death by autoerotic asphyxiation. The officers do not completely check rooms to look for signs of asphyxiation. As a result of this lack, the data is not very reliable regarding the number of deaths by autoerotic asphyxiation per year. But some specialists estimate that, "there are five hundred to one thousand autoerotic deaths every year in the United States."[52]

Personal testimonies of persons affected by this behavior help release the pain and anguish caused by the loss of loved ones. Such testimonies allow for others to talk about these situations in groups, and focus on ways of preventing more deaths. Here is one testimony:

> A good friend and neighbor died from this. He was twenty-five and had everything a kid his age could want. I wish I could send his father this information without hitting a sore spot. His father found him and cut him down before the EMTs got there and denied that this is what happened to his son. But my brother was one of the EMTs and was told by the medical examiner that all the signs were there to point to sexual asphyxiation. I hate to see the family in so much pain and being ashamed and wish I could let them know there was nothing they could have done to change things. May he always be in our memories and forever loved."[53]

The devastating affects on families is one of the major reasons why autoerotic asphyxiation deaths are often called suicides. Another testimony says:

> We are friends of a victim of this situation that occurred last month. My roommate has been successful in finding your page on the Web and referred it to me. After reading this page, we have found more answers to our enigmatic questions, and therefore we would like to show our gratitude for your research.
>
> We were not familiar with this type of activity because of its social taboo. However, when we came across the reasons for our friend's death, it has become more and more explanatory and less confusing. We are both very strong in our religion and feel it very ironic that our friend, who was religiously strong also, would deem this type of activity appropriate for his lifestyle. We understand that there are sometimes questions that can't be answered, but this has thrown us for a loop. It is still hard to fathom any solution for our friend's reasoning on this activity. We have come to accept the realism of his death, and we can only pray that more individuals of our age are confronted with this type of wrongful personal gratification and activity. Many people need to understand the very real and troubling results, and anything you can do to prevent this is appreciated. Our emotions are confused, but we understand that each person has his own lifestyle and agenda. I pray for those who are repeat experimentalists and hope that they would find a less traumatic way to replace impure desires. Our friend was a son and a brother to a very wonderful and God-fearing family. We hope that his death, as hard as it is to talk about, will be the last from this cause.[54]

As you can see, this behavior is not limited to the abnormal outcasts of society. Religious and God-fearing people have the same struggles if they allow themselves to be put in situations where they have no control, and sin overtakes their lives. So what advice can we give to people who are either struggling with this situation or they know someone who is?

First, we need to know what to look for when identifying an autoerotic death scene compared to a suicide scene. The Hazelwood report was based on a study conducted by the FBI Academy in which Roy Hazelwood and his associates studied over 125 autoerotic fatalities. They "reviewed the most important features of the autoerotic death scene and found these:

1. The location was usually secluded or private.
2. The victim's body was partially supported by the ground, floor, or other surface.
3. The most common injurious agent was a ligature.
4. The victim employed a self-rescue mechanism.
5. Bondage was a common appearance within the scenes.
6. The scene usually displayed evidence of masochism.
7. The victim was attired in one or more articles of female clothing.
8. Protective padding was frequently found between the ligature and adjacent body surface.
9. Sexual paraphernalia were located on or near the victim.

10. The victim was usually engaging in some sort of masturbatory activity.
11. The scene contained evidence of prior autoerotic experience and activity.
12. Injurious agents were complex in nature."[55]

The thought of finding a friend or family member in this scenario is heartbreaking. To combat this problem, we have different avenues of attack.

First, we need to reach out to the community and families of victims and potential victims of this behavior and get them involved in loving, caring churches. They need to know that Christ can fulfill all of their needs and nothing can fill the void like Christ. Church people need to be educated about "the dangers of hypoxia and ligature strangulation. Death is a strong deterrent."[56] People need to be aware of the situations and help individuals who are dealing with the problem. Those people who think that their loved ones are going through hard times need to seek professionals and support groups for guidance. Above all, they need our prayers and support through this difficult time in their lives.

chapter 8

Case Studies

Ever wondered what is going on in teenagers' lives? TeenHopeLine is one of the best Website resources we know of. We have worked with them over the years and have appreciated their ministry. They are on the cutting edge of technology when it comes to teenagers and the Internet. Young people take advantage of the anonymity of cyberspace and become quite candid with the TeenHopeLine staff.[1]

The following stories are summaries of actual Internet encounters. The names have been changed to secure the privacy of the teenagers. Life is complicated for them, yet, as you'll see, they found hope in faith and Scripture.

Jennifer

Nineteen-year-old Jennifer was adopted when she was a few months old. She graduated from high school, lives by herself in her parents' home, and is looking for work. She is hoping to get her driver's license so she can drive the car that was left to her. She has been a Christian since she was young but never really grasped it.

When I first started talking to her, she had never told anyone what she was going through. Her dad died when she was eight years old, and this absolutely crushed her. She had a poor relationship with her mother, and it got worse after her dad died. When she was ten years old, Jennifer discovered she had been adopted; she was very angry with her mother for not telling her. She felt as if she were a mistake. Her mother ended up sending her to a boarding school in Germany for three years. When she came home, her relationship with her mother began to grow in a positive way. But after being home for only a month, she learned that her mother had cancer and didn't have long to live. Her mother died a few months later, leaving Jennifer alone with no siblings and a broken heart. She kept everything inside and was dealing with hurt, anger, and resentment.

I encouraged her to find a Christian counselor in her area. She found a counselor and they now meeting regularly. I also assured her that she wasn't a mistake. I read Psalm 139:14–16 to her, which she found encouraging, especially verse 16, "All the days ordained for me were written in your book before one of them came to be." We talked about letting out her feelings and releasing her pain. I suggested that she write her prayers to God in a journal, so in this way, she could get everything out.

She has come a long way. She is now selling her parents' house and everything in it so she isn't constantly reminded of her past. Things are changing, and she is looking forward to the days ahead. She says that she feels much closer to God now and is putting her trust in him and telling him what she is going through.

Alexis

Alexis had a tough life growing up. She was adopted into a family that was heavily involved in the occult. Alexis had been abused physically and emotionally, especially with all of the rituals and practices her parents did to her while she was young. She couldn't go into much detail with me, because she was scared that other people would find out what had happened to her.

She came to me the first time on teenhopeline.com and shared some of what she had been through. She said that she had received Christ as her personal Lord and Savior, but now she was scared of slipping back into the occult.

I told her she needed to spend time with God on a daily basis by reading her Bible and talking with him because that's how she could grow in her personal relationship with him.

Alexis said that whenever she tried to read her Bible, she felt tormented by demons and the spiritual forces around her. She doubted her faith, and said she had been bought with blood by Satan.

I told her that Christ paid the penalty for her and she didn't need to believe Satan's lies. I then read Jeremiah 29:11, "'For I know the plans I have for you,' declares the Lord, 'plans to prosper you and not to harm you, plans to give you hope and a future.'"

She questioned me about it. Then she said she saw this counterfeit verse on her screen, "'For I know the plans I have for you,' declares the Lord, 'plans to destroy you and plans to ruin your life.'"

I asked Alexis to phone our hopeline and talk to one of our chaplains. The chaplain who was working that night informed me later that she had been through much of the same thing with Alexis. Alexis even had trouble saying "Jesus," and when she did, she stuttered because Satan had such a stronghold in her life. The chaplain then led her through a declaration we use in Freedom in Christ Ministries, which goes as follows:

> *In the name and the authority of the Lord Jesus Christ, we command Satan and all evil spirits to let go of (name) in order that (name) can be free to know and choose to do the will of God. As children of God, seated with Christ in the heavenlies, we agree that every enemy of the Lord Jesus Christ be bound to silence. We say to Satan and all of his evil workers that you cannot inflict any pain or in any way stop or hinder God's will from being done today in (name) life.*

It took Alexis a while to repeat this. We found a counselor for her in her area, and I talked with Alexis a couple of weeks later. She said she was doing well and that her relationship with God had grown. She read that declaration each time before she had her devotional, and it seemed to prevent her from being spiritually oppressed.

Nicole

Thirteen-year-old Nicole grew up in a Christian home and lived with her dad. The first time she called, she said her bedroom was haunted. She wanted to know why she was hearing voices in her head. I asked her if she was involved with anything demonic, and she told me her story. Shortly after she decided to give her life to Christ, an invisible "friend" came to her. She later found out it was a "spiritual guide" or demon. It led her further and further away from the truth she found in Christ. It showed her how to do witchcraft and other demonic things, such as spells. Nicole came back to the Lord before she called, but she was still dealing with the voices in her head. She could not sleep at night because she felt as if something was in her room.

I first asked Nicole if she was reading the Bible on a daily basis? She said she was, but she did not know what she was reading because of the voices in her head. Then I asked her if she was praying. She said she was, but the same problem occurred there too. I told her to pray out loud and ask God to clear her mind before she reads and prays. I also suggested that she and her father praise God and pray out loud in her room. Then I gave her Matthew 18:18–20: "I tell you the truth, whatever you bind on earth will be bound in heaven, and whatever you loose on earth will be loosed in heaven. Again, I tell you that if two of you on earth agree about anything you ask for, it will be done for you by my Father in heaven. For where two or three come together in my name, there am I with them."

I also asked her to pray for wisdom. James 1:5–6 says, "If any of you lacks wisdom, he should ask God, who gives generously to all without finding fault, and it will be given to him. But when he asks, he must believe and not doubt, because he who doubts is like a wave of the sea, blown and tossed by the wind." I told her that she can believe these truths because God promised them.

I told her to try to get in touch with Dave Park, author of *Stomping Out the Darkness*, by going to his Web page at www.davepark.com. Then we prayed and asked God to bind the evil presence and to loose his angels to protect her, and we asked God for wisdom.

Later Nicole called me back and told me that Dave Park was going to send her his book. The evil presence in her room was gone, but she still heard voices in her head and wondered how to get rid of them.

I told her that when she hears the voices, to respond back with truth. When Satan tempted Jesus in the desert, Jesus defeated him by quoting Scripture, and so could she. God allowed her to go through this so he could use it for her testimony to others. I gave her one last verse. John 12:27–28 says, "Now my heart is troubled, and what shall I say? 'Father, save me from this hour'? No, it was for this very reason I came to this hour. Father, glorify your name!'" Then a voice came from heaven, 'I have glorified it, and will glorify it again.'"

Andrea

When Andrea first came onto teenhopeline.com, she seemed the "perfect" Christian. Growing up in a Christian home, she didn't drink or smoke, she listened to her parents, and she did what was expected of her. Other people came to Andrea for help. From the outside, even to those closest to her, Andrea seemed to have her life all figured out.

On the inside, however, Andrea was lost and confused. She came to me with many questions about God. As we talked, I realized that she was consumed with fear and guilt. She was afraid that God would not forgive her for the things she had done, and she was also afraid of letting others know that she made mistakes. Most of all, she was afraid of others finding out about her secret sin, as she called it. Since she was young, Andrea had struggled with masturbation. She was addicted, and though she promised God many times that she would quit, she had not. Afraid that God would not forgive her for breaking her promises and ashamed of her secret addiction, Andrea withdrew from others and fell into depression.

Andrea now e-mails me a couple of times a week. She says she knew God had told her to admit to someone what she had been dealing with so she could be held accountable. She had prayed for someone to confess her sin to and felt that God brought her to me for that purpose. I encouraged her to tell a strong Christian near her about her struggles. For now, however, teenhopeline.com is the only place where she feels comfortable being open. It has been a couple of months since the last time she masturbated, and she is regaining confidence, knowing that God is faithful and that she can overcome anything with his help.

Christa

Eighteen-year-old Christa, a high school senior, is from Illinois and will soon move to the West Coast for college. She is in a family of four that appears content and loving on the outside, but the reality lurking within is a whole different story.

Christa, tall, slender, and athletic, wears a fake smile every day while performing in sports activities and at school. The Christa I know rarely wears a genuine smile and lives in emotional and spiritual turmoil. She takes multiple speed pills each day, cuts when in need of a new relief, drinks, and is promiscuous when the opportunity presents itself.

Her hatred for her father consumes and controls her. He epitomizes the word "selfish" and wears a two-faced mask almost as well as his daughter. She thinks of her dad as a hypocritical Christian in every form. She loves her mom, but they cannot understand each other because neither of them lives in reality.

My heart goes out to Christa. I continue to befriend her with great joy and hope. She is often discouraged, but God has used teenhopeline.com to help her, even though her progress is slow and sometimes discouraging. I continue to encourage her with 2 Corinthian 1:4, "[God] comforts us in all our troubles, so that we can comfort those in any trouble with the comfort we ourselves have received from God." She is in the habit of stuffing her feelings into a secret place within her, but she has come a long way with being open with me about how she feels and why. The biggest hurdle now is forgiveness, but she prays for God's help in that area.

Katy

Katy is seventeen years old and lives with her mom and alcoholic stepfather. She does not remember her own dad at all, only his first name. Her mom has lived with different men ever since Katy was a small child. In fact, her mom has been married and divorced so many times that Katy's not even sure of her mom's last name.

I first talked to Katy on teenhopeline. She came on scared because she had just found out she was two months pregnant. Her boyfriend, John, was totally supportive of her having the baby and even proposed to her. But she was having doubts about marrying him. In the past he had hit her and threatened her many times. She had grown up with men who abused her mother, and she didn't want her baby to go through that. But at the same time she was scared to tell John. She felt an obligation to marry him.

My heart went out to this girl, and I wanted to help her in any way I could. I shared with her Matthew 11:28, "Come to me, all you who are weary and burdened, and I will give you rest." This opened the door to talk about her past in the church. Her older sister took her to a church down the road every Sunday. Their grandmother told them it was the right thing to do and that God would smile on them if they went. So each week the girls walked to church and sat in the back pew. And one Sunday the pastor scolded her sister for wearing short skirts and low-cut blouses. That was the last time either of them stepped foot in a church.

I talked to Katy about forgiveness towards the church, the men in her home, and her boyfriend. I asked her to call me on the teenhopeline the next week. The night she called me, she sounded depressed with no hope at all. This time we focused on her relationship with her boyfriend. She said she was planning to marry him, and if things got too bad, she would just divorce him.

I brought up her childhood, how she felt as men came and went in her home, and asked her if she wanted to live through that again.

"No," she said.

"Well," I said, "you're going to, if you have a plan B in marriage." We talked about it for a while and again she said she would call back the following week.

When Katy called back, she said she broke up with her boyfriend, that I had helped her to see the reality of it all.

I still talk to her about every week. She now has a beautiful baby girl that she's raising on her own. She's currently visiting churches and is reading the book of John. I look forward to hear of her progress. Now she even challenges me by asking what this or that means in the Bible.

She's a great girl with a future. She has to be reminded of that every now and then, but slowly she's learning God's truth, love, and forgiveness.

Rachel

Rachel grew up in a Christian family as the middle child with two brothers. Her dad had been physically abusive in the past, and her mom was emotionally abusive and manipulative. She was entering her senior year when I began talking with her.

Rachel struggled with rejection and trust issues with those around her because of her home environment. She felt as if she didn't have a good relationship with her mom. She was afraid to talk to anyone at her church about what was going on because of her family's involvement there. She was afraid her parents would find out how she felt. She had also been on a trip with her youth group where one of her male leaders made her uncomfortable in the way he had acted toward her. This along with her dad's abuse made her afraid of males. She didn't like this unhealthy fear, but she didn't know how to deal with it. She was also dealing with depression and headaches because of the stress at home. She felt God calling her to missions, but she didn't have any support from her family in this area.

I encouraged Rachel to talk with the one youth leader she felt she could trust about the experience she had had on the youth trip. She struggled with going back to group because the other leader would be there.

Rachel had a good relationship with her aunt, and I urged her to keep talking with her about what was going on in her home life. Since her abuse issues could not be handled over the Internet, I encouraged Rachel to consider Christian counseling through her church. I also wanted someone in her area to be aware of the situation.

Rachel and I talked a lot about the psalms and how we can be honest with God about our emotions. We discussed making sure she knew how God felt about her and how much he loved her. We also talked about ways to be more comfortable around guys her age. One of her favorite scripture passages is Matthew 6:25–34, and we often talked about how she could apply those verses in her daily life, especially verse 34, "Therefore do not worry about tomorrow, for tomorrow will worry about itself."

Rachel began counseling through her church after her eighteenth birthday. She comes on teenhopeline.com to tell me what is new in her life and how her plans are shaping up for the coming year. She no longer looks in fear to what her future holds and is enrolled in a Christian college. She has shared that she is more open and can trust more people with what is truly going on in her heart. She said counseling has opened up a lot of old wounds that haven't yet been healed. This has been a difficult time for her, but the wounds are slowly healing.

Amy

Amy wanted to talk about problems with her personal quiet time. She wasn't getting anything out of it, so she felt it must not be valuable.

"I can relate to your struggle," I said, "since I've also struggled with this."

"But what can I do to strengthen my relationship with God?" she asked.

Amy read her Bible and prayed daily, yet this was not effective for her. She knew what it took to have a close relationship with God, but no one had ever explained how to have a quality devotional time and the benefits of it.

We first talked about prayer. Her prayers were to reflect her needs, as well as those things for which she was thankful. I assured her that God listens to her every prayer (see Jer. 29:12). I pointed her to several passages where God says:

- "Pray continually" and to "give thanks in all circumstances" (1 Thes. 5:17–18).
- "By prayer and petition, with thanksgiving, present your requests to God" (Phil. 4:6).
- When we pray, we should "believe and not doubt" (James 1:6).

She asked how she would do this when she felt that her prayers weren't heard or went unanswered.

I took here to the book of Joshua where God told Joshua to "be strong and very courageous" (1:7). I explained that (v. 8) we are told that our strength and courage and knowing that God is with us (v. 9) come from understanding who God is, what he has done, how he works, how he speaks to us, his promises for us, and his desires for us as we read them in the Bible.

I told her that also she needed to reflect on the times that God has been there for her, protecting, providing, and blessing her in times of need. As she seeks out the works of the Lord daily, reflecting and thanking God for them, she will find strength to pray continuously. I explained, with examples from her life, how she can find personal significance and applications from the Bible. From this, I pointed her back to Jeremiah 29:11-14, and said that it not only takes prayer but also requires her to seek God with all her heart. Amy left energized and ready to take another try at her walk with God.

In dealing with Amy, I used different Bible passages and laid out their meanings, showing how they could be woven together like a large cloth sheet. Then, I showed Amy how the Scripture could apply to her personal life, like using strings to tie the sheet to her own life, forming a parachute.

I explained to Amy that as she reflected on what God had done and continued to do for her, as well as other Christians around her, then she could see how the parachute worked. The last step was to jump out of the plane to test it out.

chapter 9

Outlines

The following outlines are intended to help you generate discussions as you help your teens live lives of extreme obedience. The outlines cover a variety of topics, but focus mainly on spiritual disciplines, such as Bible study, prayer, and Scripture memory. Please read through these, adding or subtracting information as needed. You know your teens best, so arrange these to meet their specific needs. Whatever method you choose, get talking with your youth. You can do it.

Lesson 1: Quiet Times

During quiet time, a believer meets alone with God to study, to read his Word, and to pray. This is when the Holy Spirit brings convictions to one's heart.

To help teens develop quality quiet times, have them bring the one thing from their reading that they feel God is asking them to fix (conviction) and help them write their "I will" statements and formulate action plans.

How to Have a Quiet Time

Parents or youth workers can help teenagers develop their own quiet times with these suggestions:

1. Make spending time with God a priority, make it part of their everyday lives.
2. Make the right preparation, and develop plans.
   a. Determine the best time, and guard this time.
   b. Determine the best place where they can be alone.
   c. Get key materials, a good study Bible, a pen, and a notebook to write lessons learned and prayer requests. A devotional book is helpful, but nothing replaces the Word of God.
3. Be persistent until consistent.
4. Focus on the person they are meeting with (God), rather than the habit of a quiet time.

Model of a Quiet Time

Teens can use the following to structure their time with God:

1. *Prayer*
   a. Adoration—this is a time of praising God for who he is.
   b. Confession—this is a time of asking God to forgive us for our sin.
   c. Thanksgiving—this is a time of thanking God for blessings, etc.
   d. Supplication—this is a time of request.
2. *Scripture Reading*—Read a passage of Scripture.
3. *Meditation*—Reflect on the passage, and reread if necessary.
4. *Journal/Application*—In light of this Scripture, how is the teen going to change? What are they going to do? They need to write an "I will" statement.
5. *Prayer*—Prayer of commitment, asking God to help them become the person he wants them to be. Pray for insight to specific action plans they can carry out.

Reasons for Bible Study

Second Timothy 3:16: "All scripture is God-breathed and is useful for teaching, rebuking, correcting, and training in righteousness."

1. The Bible teaches us about the characteristics of God (John 14:6).
2. The Bible rebukes (points out) sin in our lives (Eph. 4:26–31).
3. The Bible is useful for correction of error (Ps. 119:9).
4. The Bible is useful for training in righteousness (Jer. 15:16).

How to Begin: Have your teens think through a scripture or passage and then brainstorm ideas and observations by utilizing *key words*. Whenever they see these words, the teens will know what the author is trying to say. These words fall into certain categories:

- Commands/Warnings: *be, be not, do, do not, must, you will*
- Comparison: *as, like*
- Condition: *if*
- Contrasts: *but, however, nevertheless*
- Key Persons: *God, Christ, Holy Spirit*
- Key Truths: *cleansed, filled, justified*
- Processing: *might, ought, should*
- Reasons: *for, for this cause*
- Summary: *so, therefore*

Teens may also utilize the following to help them discover biblical truth: the S.P.E.C.S. method of Bible study. Is there found in this passage a:

- Sin to confess
- Promise to claim

- Example to follow
- Command to obey
- Stumbling block to avoid

Encourage your teens to journal their thoughts, discoveries, and questions from the passage. A suggested quiet time sheet can be found at the end of the outlines on page 111.

For Next Week: Have a quiet time at least four times this week. Keep a journal of them to bring next week.

Suggested Memory Verse

"Yet to all who received him, to those who believed in his name, he gave the right to become children of God" (John 1:12).

Lesson 2: Prayer

Accountability Time

Have your teens share with you if they faithfully kept their quiet times and what God taught them. They should bring their journals to show what they have written down. This is the time to discuss "I will's" and action plans.

How to Pray

Encourage your teens to cover the following four areas in their prayer time:

1. A – Adoration, praising God for who he is
2. C – Confession of sin and disobedience
3. T – Thanksgiving
4. S – Supplication, requests

Read Matthew 6:9–13 (the Lord's Prayer) together and notice that Jesus said this was how we should pray. Then allow them to make observations and to ask questions about prayer.

Challenge your teens to write their prayer requests in their journals with room to write down the answers later.

Look at Jesus' example and His instruction on prayer from the following passages. Read these passages together and talk about what can be learned from them.

- Matthew 6:5–8
- Matthew 26:39
- Mark 1:35
- John 17:1–5

End in thinking about ways their prayer lives can be better or more effective based on the above verses. If need be, have them write "I will" statements and action plans based on what they've learned.

For Next Week: Encourage your teens to continue their daily quiet time and journaling. Have them choose something that they talked about in the discussion on prayer and try to apply it to their lives.

Suggested Memory Verses

"Jesus answered, "'I am the way and the truth and the life. No one comes to the Father except through me'" (John 14:6).

"For all have sinned and fall short of the glory of God" (Rom. 3:23).

Lesson 3: Prayer (part 2)

Accountability Time

Have your teens share with you how they did that week and what God taught them. They should show what they have written down in their journals. This is the time to discuss "I wills" and action plans.

Read Ephesians 3:20–21.

Five Points of Prayer

1. Variety of Prayer: what type of prayers are there
    a.
    b.

Note: For points 2–5, look up the verse(s), and in one word, write down how it relates to the subject.

2. Frequency
    a. Luke 21:36
    b. Acts 2:42
    c. Romans 12:12
    d. Colossians 3:2
    e. 1 Thessalonians 5:17
3. Power of Prayer
    a. Matthew 5:44
    b. Luke 22:40
    c. Romans 8:26–27
    d. Ephesians 3:20–21
    e. James 5:16
4. Manner of Prayer
    a. Matthew 6:5–13
    b. John 14:13
    c. 1 Peter 4:7
    d. Ephesians 6:18
5. Objects of Prayer
    a. Romans 8:26–27
    b. Ephesians 6:18
    c. 1 Timothy 2:1–6
    d. Philippians 4:6

Lesson 4: Scripture Memory

Accountability Time

Have your teens share with you how they did that week and what God taught them. They should show what they have written in their journals. This is the time to discuss "I wills" and action plans.

How to Memorize Scripture

Encourage your teens to memorize Scripture by doing the following:

1. Write out the scripture verses on cards that they can carry with them.
2. Note the context of the scripture.
3. Read the cards while walking to class, waiting for the bus, etc.
4. Set aside regular times each day to go over the cards.
5. Memorize each verse thoroughly.
    - Write the verse over and over.
    - Whisper it to themselves throughout the day.
    - Break up long sections into shorter ones for easier memorization.

Discuss why it is important to memorize Scripture (Ps. 119:11).

For Next Week: Have your teens continue with their quiet times and journaling, then review their memory verses.

Suggested Memory Verse

"I have hidden your word in my heart that I might not sin against you" (Ps. 119:11).

Lesson 5: Scripture Memorization part 2

Accountability Time

Have your teens tell how they did that week and what God taught them. They should show what they have written down in their journals. This is the time to discuss "I wills" and action plans.

Retaining Memorized Scripture

Tell your teens how to remember (and not forget) the scripture verses they have memorized by doing the following:

1. Maintain a systematic review plan of their cards. Each bullet below is a section for their cards. So, as a verse is memorized and retained each week it then moves to the semimonthly section, then to the monthly, and so on. If they forget they simply move it back through the system.
    - Week by week
    - Semimonthly
    - Monthly
    - Quarterly
    - Semiannually
2. Be fully committed to reviewing and retaining.
3. "Pray it through." Pray the verse used in the system and then pray for retention and total recall of specific verses.

For Next Week: Have your teens continue with their quiet time and journaling. Urge them to be ready to give the previous week's memory verses along with this week's memory verse.

Memory Verse

"My son, keep my words and store up my commands within you" (Prov. 7:1).

Lesson 6: Fellowship with God

Accountability Time

Have your teens tell how they did that week and what God taught them. They should show what they have written down in their journals. This is the time to discuss "I wills" and action plans.

Read the following passage together, and talk about what the passage means. **Colossians 2:6**

How Can We Consistently Experience Fellowship with God?

Explain to your teens that all Christians need to confess their sins and receive God's forgiveness. Sin keeps us from experiencing God's love. Since we all sin, we need to receive his forgiveness for our attitudes and actions. Christ's death is the basis for forgiveness to bring us into relationship with him and for daily fellowship with him. "For Christ died for sins, once for all, righteous for unrighteous, to bring you to God. He was put to death in the body, but made alive by the Spirit" (1 Peter 3:18). Even though we are totally forgiven, we still need to deal with our sins on a day-to-day basis in order to experience continuing fellowship. When God brings to our attention some way that we've sinned, we should confess it and ask his forgiveness.

Challenge for the Week

Urge your teens to ask God to reveal any sin in their lives each day. They should write down what comes to mind on a piece of paper and be completely honest, as this is between them and God. After completing their list, they can write out 1 John 1:9 below their list, then thank God for his forgiveness, and throw the list away.

Encourage your teens to continue in their daily quiet times and journaling.

They can choose four different passages, and record what stands out to them in their journal.

Memory Verse

"Search me, O God, and know my heart; test me and know my anxious thoughts. See if there is any offensive way in me, and lead me in the way everlasting." (Ps. 139:23–24).

Just a Thought

Ask your teens these questions:

- How often do you need to confess sin to God?
- When should you confess sin?
- If you still feel guilty after you have confessed your sins, read Psalm 32:5 and Psalm 103:10–14.
- What do these passages say about guilt and cleansing?
- How will your life be affected by applying these truths?

Understanding forgiveness:

- God's forgiveness is based on his own character (Dan. 9:9,18, 19).
- God forgives us for his name's sake (Ps. 25:11; 79:9; Isaiah 43:25; 1 John 2:12).
- God is ready to forgive (Ps. 86:5; 130:3–4).
- God forgets our sin (Ps. 103:10–14; Micah 7:18–20).

Lesson 7: How We Sin, and How to Stop!

Accountability Time

Have your teens share with you how they did that week and what God taught them. They should show what they have written down in their journals. This is the time to discuss "I wills" and action plans.

This session will give students a blueprint on how to say no to sin. Have them read the passage, then fill in the blanks. The key is at the end of this lesson.

James 1:13–15

1. We _______________ wrong and _______________
   Defined: What is a wrong desire? _____________
   ____

2. We ______________________ this desire with its _______________ and then act upon it.
3. We make a _______________decision to fulfill the desire.
4. We ____________________ ourselves to the desire (we become its servant).
5. We ______________ and _______________ in this new behavior.
6. It becomes a sinful ________________ and a ____________________ sin.

Key to the questions:

1. experience; desire (anything that goes against God's Word)
2. visualize; pleasure
3. willful
4. yield
5. practice; participate
6. habit; besetting

How We Yield to God and Turn from Sin:

1. We experience a prompting/conviction from the _________________ and _______________ our sin.
2. We _________________ the action necessary to _______________ the conviction work toward _________________ the habit.
3. We envision the __________________ and the __________________ we will experience with victory over the besetting sin.
4. We make a ______________ decision to __________ the conviction.
5. We __________________ to God.

Key:

1. Holy Spirit; acknowledge
2. visualize; obey; breaking
3. fulfillment; satisfaction
4. willful; obey
5. surrender

Lesson 8: Sharing Jesus with Others

This lesson will cover witnessing, what it is, why we should do it, and how to do it. People love to share good news with others. The more exciting the news, the harder it is to keep silent. As Christians, we have the most exciting news, the life-changing news of eternal life. Think about who led you to the Lord. Aren't you thankful he or she was obedient to God and witnessed to you?

Why Do We Witness?

- God commanded it!
  "He said to them, 'Go into all the world and preach the good news to all creation'" (Mark 16:15).

How Do We Witness?

- You can include your personal testimonies as to what you were like before you met Christ, what happened when you accepted him as Savior, and what you are like now.
- Scripture: These verses are considered the "Roman's Road" to salvation. Follow the verses in a systematic way to lead people to Christ.
  Romans 1:16; 2:4; 3:23; 5:8; 6:4, 23; 8:16–17, 35–39; 10:9,13–14;12:1–2; 15: 4–6, 13.

Our Objective

We should move people from a pointless faith to a faith that points to God.

Personal Devotions

Use the following chart to journal your Bible reading and quite times. As you read, look for the following in the passage: is there a sin to watch out for, a promise to claim, an example to follow, a command to keep, and/or a stumbling block (things that can slow us down or trip us up in our walk with Christ) to avoid?

Personal Devotions

PASSAGE:____________________

DATE:______________

	YES	NO	VERSE
SIN			
PROMISE			
EXAMPLE			
COMMAND			
STUMBLING BLOCK			

Important Verse or Phrase:

____
____
____
____
____
____

Personal Application:

____
____
____
____
____

chapter **10**

Internet Resources

http://www.aacap.org/

This site is designed to serve American Academy of Child and Adolescent Psychiatry members, parents, and families. Information is provided as a public service to aid in the understanding and treatment of developmental, behavioral, and mental disorders that affect an estimated seven to twelve million children and adolescents at any given time in the United States. You will find information on child and adolescent psychiatry, fact sheets for parents and caregivers, AACAP membership, current research, practice guidelines, managed-care information, awards and fellowship descriptions, meeting information, and much more. Since no child and adolescent psychiatrists are on staff, it is neither ethical nor responsible to give consultations for specific children and families.

http://www.acf.dhhs.gov/index.html

Maintained by the U.S. Department of Health and Human Services, this site includes profiles of America's youth, reports, stats, publications, and speeches on youth topics. It includes a list of resources for parents and links to related sites.

http://www.adcouncil.org/

It's the Ad Council's mission is to identify a select number of significant public issues and to stimulate action through communications programs that make a measurable difference in society. To that end, the Ad Council marshals volunteer talent from the advertising and communications industries, the facilities of the media, and the resources of the business and nonprofit communities to create awareness, foster understanding, and motivate action.

http://www.advocatesforyouth.org/

Established in 1980 as the Center for Population Options, Advocates for Youth champion efforts to help young people make informed and responsible decisions about their reproductive and sexual health. Advocates believe it can best serve the field by boldly advocating for a positive and realistic approach to adolescent sexual health. Advocates for Youth is the only organization that works both in the United States and in developing countries with a sole focus on adolescent reproductive and sexual health.

http://www.afterschool.gov/

What can our federal government do for teens? Do they need to do research in science, history, art, music, political science? Are they interested in volunteer and employment opportunities? Do they need Social Security cards? Are they searching for careers? Do they need financial aid for college? This site provides a gateway to federal and other publicly supported Websites for teens. They can find information to help them do their homework, pursue hobbies, choose careers, or have fun. The site is supported by the General Services Administration.

http://www.allprodad.com

All Pro Dad is the ultimate resource for men who want to become better fathers. This program offers practical fathering assistance. It is updated daily and is available twenty-four hours a day, 365 days a year. The All Pro Dad website's premier offering is a free daily e-mail service called Play of the Day. This service provides dads with hard-hitting information, advice, and inspiration to make them better husbands and fathers.

All Pro Dad features NFL players and coaches who want to make men better fathers. In addition, All Pro Dad is impacting communities by bringing fathers and their kids together for All Pro Dads' Day. This website also offers fathers interactive quizzes and activities designed to further improve their relationship with their children. At allprodad.com, fathers can also find books, brochures, free articles, online classes, surveys, support groups, and many other resources on parenting.

http://www.boundless.org/

The time between the home of your youth and the home you'll make for yourself someday is full of adventure, discovery, and excitement but also loneliness, longing, and uncertainty.

From college to career to relationships, people at Boundless want to cast a vibrant vision for the single years, helping teens navigate this season while preparing for the challenges and responsibilities ahead. That requires teens living intentionally with purpose by bringing their gifts, talents, and Christian worldviews to bear on their whole lives. Contributing authors are renowned journalists, scholars, and thinkers from around the globe who help teens enjoy the journey.

http://www.briomag.com/

Brio is an Italian word that means "full of energy, life and enthusiasm." It's the name of a magazine for teen girls because it's a terrific definition of its readers. For more than 13 years, *Brio* has been teaching, entertaining, and challenging girls toward healthy self-concepts and closer relationships with Jesus Christ.

http://www.campuslife.net

Campus Life.net is a division of *Christianity Today* magazine. This site is ideal for teens who are looking for information on various topics with advice and resources at hand. Personal testimonies and real-life stories show that they are not alone in their problems. Campus Life even has a helpful college guide for those teens who are struggling with choosing the right college or university.

http://www.cfw.tufts.edu

Due to the expanding volume of information on the Web, parents and professionals often have difficulty locating the information they want. Even when they find information that seems relevant, they have difficulty determining if it is credible. The Child & Family Web Guide describes trustworthy websites on topics of interest to parents and professionals. All the sites listed on the Web Guide have been systematically evaluated by graduate students and faculty in child development. These sites have been selected from thousands available on the Web, based primarily on the quality of the information they provide. The goal of the Web Guide is to give the public easy access to the best child-development information on the Web.

Five primary categories of information are provided: family/parenting, education/learning, typical child development, health/mental health, and resources/recreation. The first four categories contain sites with research-based information. The fifth category (resources/recreation) contains sites with information about specific programs and things to do. The resources/recreation sites, which were added at the request of parents, do not contain research-based information. The Web Guide also offers an option of searching for sites relevant to particular age groups, as well as several features requested by parents (e.g., ask-an-expert sites; research-news sites).

http://www.childrensdefense.org/

This site is sponsored by a Children's Defense Fund, a non-profit organization whose mission it is to "leave no child behind and to ensure every child a healthy start, a head start, a fair start, a safe start, and a moral start in life and successful passage to adulthood with the help of caring families and communities."

http://www.childstats.gov/

This is the official site of the Federal Interagency Forum on Child and Family Statistics. It provides access to federal and state statistics and reports on children and their families. It is a good source for current demographic statistics on today's youth culture.

http://www.christiananswers.net/teens/home.html

This mega-site provides biblical answers to contemporary questions for all ages and nationalities with over thirty thousand files. It is a faith ministry of Eden Communications.

http://www.christianstudents.com/

Through the relationships developed over the past several years with Gospelcom.net and Youth Specialties, the DreamStar Group presented the idea of a Christian community for teens. Many thanks should go to Youth Specialties for adopting the vision and presenting it to Gospelcom. Thanks should also go to Youth for Christ and everybody who contributes content for ChristianStudents.com. This site is dedicated to Christian teens who are looking for answers to all their questions.

http://www.confidentparenting.com/

Confident Parenting Today had its beginnings in conversations with the thousands of parents across the country who came to seminars led by children-and-family-life specialist Richard Patterson Jr. These parents had many questions. Some felt intimidated by the challenges they faced and had lost confidence to act decisively as parents on behalf of their children. Other parents, however, learned how to be confident, successful parents through hard work, prayer, and experience. Passing their wisdom on to parents who wanted it became the genesis of Confident Parenting Today.

http://www.cpyu.org

The Center for Parent/Youth Understanding is a nonprofit organization building strong families by bridging the cultural-generational gap between parents and teenagers. At a time when youth culture is changing quickly, CPYU helps parents, youth workers, and educators understand teenagers and their culture so they will be better equipped to help teens navigate the challenging world of adolescence.

The mission of CPYU is to work with churches, schools, and community organizations to build stronger relationships between young people and those charged with helping them grow into healthy adulthood. This mission is accomplished by:

- Helping parents understand and respond to the complex world of their children and teens from a distinctively Christian point of view.

- Equipping teenagers to deal with the challenges of adolescence.
- Equipping parents and teens to respond to these challenges through a distinctive Christian worldview.
- Raising the youth-culture awareness of youth workers and educators, thereby helping them increase their effectiveness with parents and teens.

http://www.cybertipline.com/

Cyber Tip Line is part of the National Center for Missing and Exploited Children. Besides being a place to report leads about missing and exploited children, the website also offers valuable tips for parents, teens, and children Internet users on how to stay safe online.

http://www.drugfree.org/

Created and maintained by the Partnership for a Drug-Free America, this site offers a complete and accurate compilation of information about substance abuse. Included is a comprehensive database on drugs and help for parents.

http://www.family.org/

The goal of this Focus on the Family site is to disseminate the gospel of Jesus Christ to as many people as possible to help preserve traditional values and the institution of the family.

From humble and simple beginnings—a book on child discipline and a twenty-five minute weekly broadcast that first aired in 1977—Focus on the Family has grown over the years to include a wide array of separate ministries under its umbrella.

http://www.familyeducation.com/home/

Launched in 1996 as the first parenting site on the Web, Family Education has become the Internet's most visited site for parents who are involved, committed, and responsive to their families' needs.

Parents find practical guidance, grade-specific information about their children's school experiences, strategies to get involved with their children's learning, free e-mail newsletters, and entertaining family activities. Family Education brings together leading organizations from both the public and private sectors to help parents, teachers, schools, and community organizations use online tools and other media resources to positively affect children's education and overall development.

http://www.focusas.com/

Focus Adolescent Services is an Internet clearinghouse of information and resources to help support families with troubled and at-risk teens.

Its mission is to provide information and resources to empower individuals to help their teens and heal their families. Through education, self-awareness, self-help, and personal responsibility, families can rebuild their relationships in positive and loving ways. The free availability of the Focus Website reflects a commitment to disseminate knowledge to the widest possible audience. Professionals, journalists, youth workers, and students also find valuable information at Focus Adolescent Services to help them in their work and study.

http://www.freevibe.com/

Freevibe.com is a site constructed for teens by the National Youth Anti-Drug Media Campaign but is worthy of some study by those working with young people. The site's major theme is anti-drug information, stories, and discussion. It lists information on common drugs and effects, as well as stories about bad drug experiences, pop culture, and media literacy.

http://www.health.org/

The National Clearinghouse for Alcohol and Drug Information (NCADI) is the nation's one-stop resource for information about substance-abuse prevention and addiction treatment. This online parents' guide to youth culture comes from the Department of Health and Human Services. It also includes helpful information on changes in youth culture, the power of music, and media literacy.

http://www.nichd.nih.gov/default.htm

The National Institute of Child Health and Human Development (NICHD) is part of the National Institutes of Health, the biomedical research arm of the U.S. Department of Health and Human Services Department of Health and Human Services. The mission of the NICHD is to ensure that babies are born healthy and wanted, that women suffer no harmful effects from reproductive processes, and that all children have the chance to achieve their full potential for healthy and productive lives, free from disease or disability. The department also wants to ensure the health, productivity, independence, and well-being of all people through optimal rehabilitation.

http://www.parenting-love-is-the-answer.com/index.html

This website is dedicated to providing more than just information and resources for parents. Within each topic is a "love prescription." These comments are intended to create a loving perspective of the particular topic. The "love prescription" is designed to remind parents to include love in their relationships with their children.

http://www.parentskidsdirectory.com/index.php

Parents and Kids Directory is a very thorough site filled with numerous resources for a large variety of issues pertaining to parenting.

http://www.passageway.org/

This streamlined site is an outreach of the Billy Graham Evangelical Association. A question-and-answer page is offered where users can send questions to be answered by Passageway staff. Links offer archived discussions of spiritual and lifestyle resources, ranging from topics on attending church to suicide. Christians serving in the arts are also profiled.

http://www.planetwisdom.com/

This website from Wisdom Works Ministries is designed to help students live from God's perspective. It includes thoughtful and biblical reviews of movies, music, television, and other aspects of the culture, providing great discussion starters for youth groups or Bible studies.

http://www.ransomfellowship.org/

Ransom Fellowship is the writing/speaking ministry of Denis and Margie Haack. This site reflects the ministry's mission to help Christians develop skills of discernment and deepen their discipleship. The site offers helpful foundational material, as well as numerous reviews of books, films, etc.

http://www.realfamilies.com/

Reality Talks! provides Christian parenting advice from Dr. Kevin Leman and Dr. Jay Passavant. It includes parenting tips and information categorized by children's ages, along with resources for marriage.

http://www.search-institute.org/

Search Institute is an independent, nonprofit organization providing leadership, knowledge, and resources to promote healthy children, youth, and communities. To accomplish this mission, the institute communicates new knowledge and brings together community, state, and national leaders.

http://www.summit.org

Summit Ministries is an educational Christian ministry that is a response to the current post-Christian culture. Countless Christian young people are renouncing their faith and adopting the false humanistic philosophies of today.

Summit views its role as a catalyst to counteract this alarming trend. As Christians are challenged to stand strong in their faith and to defend truth, they will also have a positive influence on the society in which they live.

http://www.teenhopeline.com/

The goal of this site is to reach teenagers with the good news of Jesus Christ. It enables teens to talk with staff members about their problems.

http://www.thecommunityofconcern.org/

In 1998, in response to a need, parents from Georgetown Preparatory School in Bethesda, Maryland, wrote and published a booklet, *A Parent's Guide for the Prevention of Alcohol, Tobacco and Other Drug Use.*

The overwhelming positive response to the booklet by families at Georgetown Prep led James Power, Headmaster, and Mimi Fleury—parent and chair of the Substance-Abuse Manual Committee and former president of the parents' board—to form the Community of Concern consortium. When the consortium shared the booklet with other Washington, D.C. schools, the response was amazing. By February 2000, thousands of copies had been delivered to thirty-two area schools and the Parent's Council of Washington.

http://www.troubledteen101.com/

Troubled Teen 101 is presented for parents in need of help with their teens. The site offers information on teen issues, problems, and behavior disorders. It recommends programs for troubled teens, boarding schools, and boot-camp alternatives, as well as information regarding military schools, boot camps, and wilderness programs. This organization promotes home-based solutions and long-term options.

http://www.understandingyourteenager.com/

The first Understanding Your Teenager seminar was created and presented in 1988 by Youth Specialties. The seminar provided a quality training event to help church youth workers minister more effectively to parents of teens in their groups.

After two years, Youth Specialties discontinued the UYT seminar program, but YS cofounder Wayne Rice kept it going on his own with the help of several new team members. Together they revised and further developed the seminar content to help and encourage parents of teenagers.

In 1994, Rice left Youth Specialties and formed Understanding Your Teenager as an independent organization to serve parents of preteens and teens as well as youth workers. Since then, UYT has conducted more than one thousand seminars and continues to be a leader in the field of youth and family ministry.

http://www.wholefamily.com/indexIE.html

The Whole Family Community site provides the tools and advice to parents, teens, couples, or seniors that are needed to build strong, healthy, loving relationships. A team of experts and professionals offer real-life solutions for today's tough challenges.

http://www.youthdevelopment.org/

The Institute of Youth Development (IYD) is a nonpartisan, nonprofit organization promoting a comprehensive avoidance message to youth for harmful risk behaviors that are linked: alcohol, drugs, sex, tobacco, and violence. The site is designed for professionals, parents, and teens.

http://www.yfc.net/Brix?pageID=2941

The vision of Youth for Christ is to see young people in every nation have the opportunity to make informed decisions to become followers of Jesus Christ and part of local churches. This involves responsible evangelism of youth, presenting them with the person, work, and teachings of Christ and discipling them into local churches.

http://www.youthspecialties.com

For over 30 years, Youth Specialties has worked alongside Christian youth workers of most denominations and youth-serving organizations. This organization helps both brand-new and veteran youth ministers, as well as volunteer workers with youth. Each year they serve more than one hundred thousand youth workers worldwide through their training seminars, conventions, resources, and on the Internet.

http://www.zjam.com/

ZJAM Youth Ministries is committed to reaching students around the world through the means of ZJAM radio,

Internet Bible studies, websites, mission trips, and youth rallies. Its goal is to reach teenagers with the good news of Jesus Christ.

Notes

Chapter 1: What a Teenager Looks Like

1. Karen Peterson, "For Parents, Advice Overkill," USA Today McLean, Va.: Oct 30, 2002, D.06.

Chapter 5: Boundaries

1. Judith Rich Harris, *The Nurture Assumption: Why Children Turn Out the Way They Do* (Free Press: New York, 1998)

Chapter 6: Modeling

1. Oswald Chambers, *My Utmost for His Highest* (N.Y.: Dodd, Mead, 1963), 131.
2. Jerry Jenkins, *Twelve Things I Want My Kids to Remember* (Chicago: Moody Press, 1991), 29–30.
3. Ross Campbell, *Relational Parenting* (Chicago: Moody Press, 2000), 138.
4. Martha Miller, "6 Secrets to Raising a Successful Teen." *Better Homes and Gardens*, October, 1998.

Chapter 7: Issues

1. Special thanks to Kristen Speck, Josh Sillaman, James Fay, Brian Greer, Alethea Riddle, Jessica Weber, Brendan Allison, and Jonathan R. Morrow for their research and writing on the issues discussed in this chapter.
2. http://supak.com/sunscreen.htm

3. Vukich, Lee and Vandegriff, Steve. *Timeless Youth Ministry* (Chicago: Moody Press, 2000), 103.
4. "The Sexual Shadows—Trends" *Group* magazine, January 2, 2004.
5. http://www.womensenews.org/article.cfm/dyn/aid/1580.
6. "Privacy" *Teen People*, May 2005.
7. "Celeb Gossip" *Teen People*, May 2005.
8. http://www.seventeen.com.
9. http://www.tenessean.com/features/health/archives/05/01/65356499.shtml?Element_ID65356499.
10. http://www.usdoj.gov/ndic/pubs07/708.
11. http://www.usdoj.gov/ndic/pubs07/708.
12. http://www.phillyburbs.com/couriertimes/news/huffing.
13. http://www.connectwithkids.com.
14. http://www.teamcare.org.
15. http://www.parentsroom.org.
16. http://www.halifaxherald.com/external/abusedparents/abusedparents.html.
17. http://ladyria.us/causes/parent_abuse.html.
18. Of that 51%, 45.7% reported using marijuana, 10% inhalants, 4.6% LSD, 3.9% crack-cocaine, 8.1% cocaine, and 1.5% heroin. This test was funded by the NIDA, and conducted by the University of Michigan's Institute for Social Research.
19. http://www.publicagenda.org/issues/factfiles_detail.cfm?issue_type=illegal_drugsc-list=9.
20. Tracey, Scott. "Two Men Stabbed Over Drugs, 3 Men in Custody." *Guelph Mercury*, 15 Jan. 2005; final ed.
21. Stockwell, Jamie. "Teen Dies in Shooting, Drug Related." *The Washington Post*, 22 Sept. 2004; final ed.
22. Ibid.
23. http://www.NIDA.nih.gov/drugpages.
24. http://www.NIDA/Infofax/HSYouthtrends.
25. Ibid.
26. Identity theft occurs "when someone steals your name, address or other personal information and uses it for their financial gain." In essence, the thief takes on the identity of

the person that the identity was stolen from (qwest). First came phishing scams, in which con artists hooked unwary Internet users one by one into compromising their personal data. Now the latest cyberswindle, pharming, threatens to reel in entire schools of victims. Pharmers simply redirect as many users as possible from the legitimate commercial websites they'd intended to visit and lead them to malicious ones. The bogus sites, to which victims are redirected without their knowledge or consent, will likely look the same as genuine sites. But when users enter their login names and passwords, the information is captured by criminals. "Phishing is to pharming what a guy with a rod and a reel is to a Russian trawler. Phishers have to approach their targets one by one. Pharmers can scoop up many victims in a single pass," said Chris Risley, president and chief executive officer of Nominum, a provider of IP address infrastructure technology for businesses. http://www.wired.com/news/infostructure/0,1377,66853,00.html.

27. http://www.cbsnews.com/stories/2001/05/15/60II/main291415.shtml.
28. http://computer.howstuffworks.com/identity-theft.htm.
29. Ibid.
30. http://www.qwest.com/highwayqwest/identitytheft.
31. Ibid.
32. Ibid.
33. http://www.wnbc.com/money/2682876/detail.html.
34. http://www.pestpatrol.com/Support/About/About_Key Loggers.asp.
35. http://www.nasd.com/web/idcplg?IdcService=SS_GET_PAGE&ssDocName=NASDW_010734.
36. http://www.state.ny.us/governor/press/year02/oct9_02.htm. "The new law criminalized identity theft and the unlawful possession of personal identification information to commit fraud or other criminal acts and enables victims to secure restitution for their losses."
37. http://www.crime-research.org/news/2003/01/Mess0802.htm.

38. http://www.kidzworld.com/site/p33-11.htm.
39. http://www.phac-aspc.gc.ca/publicat/cdic-mcc/17-2/b_e.html.
40. http://www.focusas.com.
41. Jeff Weise also made a flash short film that was very bloody, posted on the website, http://www.thesmokinggun.com/archive/0323051weise1.html.
42. The Website: http://cryptome.org/jeff-weise2.htm, has the story Jeff Weise wrote. It is supposed to be part of a three-part series. The writings were collected on March 25, 2005.
43. http://www.focusas.com.
44. Haskins, Cora. "Treating Sibling Incest Using a Family Approach," *Journal of Mental Health Counseling*, Oct 2003, Vol. 25, Issue 4.
45. http://www.psychpage.com/family/library/sib_abuse.htm Niolon, Richard. *Sibling Sexual Abuse*, Dec. 2000.
46. Haskins, Cora. "Treating Sibling Incest Using a Family Approach," *Journal of Mental Health Counseling*, Oct 2003, Vol. 25, Issue 4.
47. http://www.psychpage.com/family/library/sib_abuse.htm Niolon, Richard. *Sibling Sexual Abuse*, Dec. 2000.
47. Goad, Ben. "Siblings Accused of Incest." Press Enterprise, 25 June 2003.
48. http://www.answers.com/topic/autoerotic-asphyxiation.
49. http://www.psychdirect.com/forensic/Criminology/para/aea.htm.
50. http://www.silentvictims.org/.
51. http://www.answers.com/main/ntquery;jsessionid=1ms8c70o51d1f?method=4&dsid=2222&dekey=Autoerotic+fatalities&gwp=8&curtab=2222_1&sbid=lc03b.
52. http://www.silentvictims.org/correspond.htm.
53. Ibid.
54. http://www.law-forensic.com/autoerotic_2.htm.
55. http://www.silentvictims.org/FAQ's.htm.

Chapter 8: Case Studies

56. Special thanks to Graham, Jennifer, Josh, Marisa, Natasha, Nicole, Shoni, and Tim of the TeenHopeLine staff.

disturbing
behavior
53
alarming
trends
of teens